STEER
THROUGH
THE
STORM

How to Communicate and Lead Courageously Through Change

LEAH METHER

First published in 2023 by Methmac Communications Pty Ltd.
All rights reserved.

No part of this publication may be reproduced by any means without written prior consent of the publisher.

This book uses personal stories and examples from clients to highlight key points. Names have been changed to protect individual privacy.

Every effort has been made to trace and acknowledge the original source of material used within this book. Where the attempt has been unsuccessful, the publisher would be pleased to hear from the author/publisher to rectify any omission.

Edited by Lu Sexton.
Proofread by Stephanie Preston.
Book coach: Kath Walters.
Typeset by Liz Seymour, Seymour Designs.

Printed and bound by Ingram Sparks.

National Library of Australia Cataloguing-in-Publication entry

Title: Steer Through the Storm

Subtitle: How to Communicate and Lead Courageously Through Change

ISBN: 978-0-6484845-2-3 (paperback)
ISBN: 978-0-6484845-3-0 (e-book)

Subjects: Business, communication, leadership, emotional intelligence, change leadership, soft skills.

Other creators/contributors: Sexton, Lu, editor; Seymour, Liz, designer; Walters, Kath, book coach.

PRAISE FOR STEER THROUGH THE STORM

"In *Steer Through the Storm*, author Leah Mether has once again delivered an exceptional book that is both insightful and instructive, packed with inspiring personal stories, case studies, and actionable insights. This book is a must-read for any leader responsible for implementing change and ensuring that their team is their best selves through the process. Leah's insights are invaluable and her writing style is engaging, making this book an essential addition to any leader's toolkit."

Janine Garner, International speaker, 3 x bestselling author, CEO Curious Minds Aus Pty Ltd, business mentor and host of *Unleashing Brilliance* podcast

"*Steer Through the Storm* is the book I wish I'd had in my 30s. As a relatively young senior leader, I found myself in some sticky situations dealing with 'people stuff' in the midst of major organisational change. The change was outside my control – but my behaviour and intentions were not. People lean into leadership best when they use and manage their emotions to the best effect – and when they read and understand the emotions projected by the people around them. This book will help you do that. Whether you are steamrolling, shirking or steering, you need to comprehend how you are showing up and how that impacts your team and you. As the role of leaders continues to evolve more rapidly than at any other time in the history of work, this is the book we need. Leah Mether has written a practical resource for relationships of rigour."

Maree McPherson OAM, Leadership trainer, coach and mentor, Founder and Director The Grass Ceiling Pty Ltd, author of *Cutting Through the Grass Ceiling*, **and** *Worthy* – shortlisted in the Australian Business Book Awards 2022

"Leah has delivered another phenomenally helpful resource jam-packed with practical, actionable guidance for leaders navigating the bumpy waters of change on a journey not of their choosing. Peppered with the right questions to be asking and answering, *Steer Through The Storm* is a fabulous gift to leaders in our volatile, uncertain, complex and ambiguous world."

Tanya Heaney-Voogt, Mentally Healthy Workplaces Expert and Workplace Change Facilitator, author of *Transforming Norm – Leading the Change to a Mentally Healthy Workplace*, and lead Mentally Healthy Workplaces - The Australian Transformation & Turnaround Association

PRAISE FOR SOFT IS THE NEW HARD

"This book is a masterclass in communication. Packed with case studies, stories and research, it has a perfect blend of anecdote and data. Soft is indeed the new hard, and sometimes it's real hard. But as Leah has shown with succinct and elegantly simple concepts, it's a skill that can be learned. Full of many eye-opening, 'wow!' moments and many more reassuring 'phew, it's not just me' moments, this isn't just a book for leaders, it's a book for life."

Rachael Robertson, Antarctic expedition leader, leadership expert and author of *Leading on the Edge*

"If you are a leader who wants to be heard in the 21st century, this book decodes the future of communications."

Oscar Trimboli, Author of *How to Listen: Discover the Hidden Key To Better Communication* and *Deep Listening: Impact Beyond Words*, award-winning podcaster of *Deep Listening* and keynote speaker

"As Roger Enrico, Pepsi's former CEO, so aptly observed, 'It's the soft stuff that's hard,' – and that is exactly at the heart and soul of Leah Mether's *Soft is the New Hard*. Leah brings the lessons of her experience and offers great insight and advice on overcoming the challenges of constructive communication. This is a 'must read' for anyone who desires to transform drama into empowerment in the relationships that matter most!"

David Emerald, Author *The Power of TED* (*The Empowerment Dynamic)* **and** *3 Vital Questions: Transforming Workplace Drama*

"In *Soft is the New Hard*, Leah has created a very practical guide that gives all of us the opportunity to become more effective communicators under pressure. Being aware of what drives and motivates us and influences our choices in communication enables all of us to step into a conversation in a very different way. Understanding our own impact and taking 'control' of the choices we make and the way in which we engage others creates very different outcomes – ones that enable us to move forward and remain 'above the line'. The compelling stories that she shares throughout the book and the practical examples offered for us to test and explore also make this content very real and current. We are looking forward to continuing to use it ourselves and recommending it to others."

Gayle Hardie and **Malcolm Lazenby**, Co-founders, Global Leadership Foundation

ABOUT THE AUTHOR

Leah Mether is a communication specialist obsessed with making the people part of leadership and work life easier.

She is a speaker, trainer, mentor and author known for her practical, relatable, straight-shooting style.

With a background in leadership, corporate communications and journalism, Leah works with leaders and teams across Australia to help them self-manage under pressure, defuse conflict, build relationships of influence and communicate effectively.

Her work is based on the belief that "soft" skills get hard results and no one is a perfect communicator, everyone can improve.

Leah's first book *Soft is the New Hard: How to Communicate Effectively Under Pressure* was a finalist in the Australian Career Book of the Year Awards in 2020.

She lives in the small town of Willow Grove in Gippsland, Victoria, overlooking Blue Rock Lake and the Baw Baw ranges, and is the mother of three energetic sons.

DEDICATION

To my family and friends who helped me steer through my own storm of change while writing this book.

And to my boys – Sam, Callum and Lucas.

CONTENTS

Introduction   xiii

PART 1 **WHY**   1

Chapter 1 **LEADING THROUGH CHANGE**   3
More heart, less head   4
The Five Cs of communicating and leading courageously
    through change   7
Lead yourself first   10
Leadership is about people; management is about tasks   11
You don't have to like the change to lead people through it   12
Anyone can lead through change   15
The stronger your relationships, the easier it is to lead
    your people through change   17

Chapter 2 **CAN'T THEY JUST GET ON WITH IT?**   20
Change is challenging   21
Resistance is real and has reasons   24
Avoidance makes problems grow   29
Organisations don't change, people do   32
Dealing with the feeling isn't optional if you want
    your change to be successful   34

Chapter 3 **DEALING WITH THE FEELING**   35
The difference between emotions, feelings and moods   36
Expect emotion, prepare for feelings   38

EQ is the new IQ 39

Common responses to change 40

There's no "one-size-fits-all" response 44

The reaction does not necessarily correspond
with the emotion underpinning it 46

Allow yourself to feel 49

Increase your emotional vocabulary 50

Emotional contagion 53

What's it like to be around me? 55

Chapter 4 **COURAGEOUS LEADERSHIP
BALANCES WARMTH AND STRENGTH** **60**

It starts with you 62

Are you in or are you out? 64

Look after yourself 67

Lead with warmth first, strength second 70

You're not a magician, you can't do it for them 73

Vulnerability is strength, not weakness 75

PART 2 **HOW** **79**

Chapter 5 **CREATE CLARITY** **80**

Get clear yourself 83

Provide clarity for your team 85

Bad news is better than no news 88

A four-part framework for communicating in uncertainty 90

What if you can't share the reasons behind a change? 93

Know your audience: it's about them, not you 94

Pre-empt curly questions with Q&A sparring 99

Questions to consider (and answer) in your messaging 100

Emphasise the why 101

Give it to them straight 104

Be proactive 105

Keep it simple 105

Tell stories   106

Own the message   107

Be clear about what people can and can't influence   111

Give them options: people don't like being told what to do   113

Chapter 6 **CONNECT WITH CURIOSITY**   **116**

Get curious with yourself   121

Empathy is essential   123

Empathy as a tool for de-escalating conflict   126

Injecting empathy is simple but incredibly powerful   128

Get curious not furious   129

Curiosity in practice   132

Ask great questions (note: "any questions?" Is not one of them)   134

Curiosity requires the courage to accept feedback well   136

Chapter 7 **CHALLENGE WITH CANDOUR**   **141**

Challenge focus   144

Challenge ethos/mindsets   148

Challenge unfettered optimism   160

Challenge behaviours   164

Challenge group think and the squeaky wheel   170

Chapter 8 **COACH WITH COMPASSION**   **179**

The most compassionate people have boundaries   186

The straw that breaks the camel's back –
    change fatigue is real   188

Make time to meet   189

Different strokes for different folks   192

The dos and don'ts of good coaching conversations   195

Don't be tempted to problem-solve, sometimes
    people just want you to listen   199

What to do when they're not ok   200

Chapter 9 **COMMIT WITH CONSISTENCY**   **206**

More than words   208

Don't lie to yourself   210

Communicate early, communicate often   214

Consistency creates calm   218

Consistent doesn't mean fixed   219

Catch people doing the right thing, and tell them   220

Celebrate the wins – big and small   222

Conclusion   226

WANT TAILORED SUPPORT?   231

Acknowledgements   232

INTRODUCTION

This book is a love letter to leaders around the world who find themselves having to steer their people through the storm of uncertainty and change.

Think industry transitions, power station shutdowns, corporate takeovers, major restructures, funding cuts, government regulations, the impacts of natural disasters, pandemics and a changing climate.

You may not have instigated it, you may not be able to control it, you may not even know what it is yet – but change is happening anyway.

And you're in the middle of it. The one who must lead people through it, even though it may not be what you signed up for, it feels like there is no "win" in it for you or your team, and you're just as uncertain as anyone about what the future will bring.

You're outside your comfort zone, can feel the tension rising in yourself and your team, and you're unsure how on earth you're going to lead your people through.

Hell, you might not even be sure how you're going to stay afloat.

If this sounds like you, take a deep breath. Shake out your arms. Roll your shoulders. You're in safe hands. I've written this book for you: the leader who has to navigate the rough seas of change without losing people overboard or sinking the ship.

You're responsible for your team adopting or adapting to the change but you may not be the one leading the change itself.

In fact, it's likely you are the piggy in the middle – your board, boss or the government is driving the change, and your people are resistant, fearful and angry. Perhaps you're even resistant, fearful and angry too! You want to yell "Don't shoot the messenger!" every time you have to deliver more change news and you're copping it from above and below.

That said, you are a professional. Part of your role as a leader is to not only be the messenger but to also own the message of change. And, even in the face of the challenge change brings, you still need a functioning team. You still have to get the job done, deliver the goals and KPIs, manage performance and behaviour, protect the safety and wellbeing of your people, and get yourself through with your own health and integrity intact.

But how do you do that? How do you lead your people through significant change – whether it comes out of left field or is years in the making? And whether you're the one driving it or not?

That's what this book is all about. Helping you lead yourself and your people THROUGH change.

Let me be clear: this is NOT a book about change project management. It's not about processes, policies, procedures and Gantt charts. It's about people and how to steer them through the storm of change to calmer waters safely and pointing in the right direction. Less of the head, more of the heart.

It's not an academic book, rather it's a practical, plain-speak guide to help you navigate your team through the rough waters in a way that steadies the ship and keeps you on course.

Many leaders find themselves the bearers of change news without ever being taught the foundations of HOW to lead their people through change. They are essentially set up to fail. While the upper echelons of an organisation will often invest in change management support for themselves, there is a gap in support for the middle management, team leader and coordinator level who actually have to get the change across the line. There is also a gap in the advice and support available for those facing change that is not of their own design, or is out of their control. It is those gaps that this book seeks to address.

I don't need to know the exact change you're going through to teach you the principles that will help you through. This book is about the foundational communication, leadership and people skills you need to support your team through any change – be it big or small. It's about feelings and emotions – but not in a light, fluffy way.

It will show you how to work with and respond to the feelings of your people in a way that allows you to influence, motivate and unite your team.

Who am I to write this book? Good question. I'm an Australian communication specialist obsessed with making the people part of leadership easier. I do this by helping leaders develop their "soft skills", which are really hard. Skills like communication, emotional intelligence, collaboration and self-management.

I've worked with thousands of leaders and teams across the country who are experiencing significant change. Leaders and teams in the power, water, government, environment, health, education, disability and aged-care sectors, some of which are under great pressure and strain. First in my role as a news journalist, then as a corporate communications manager, and for the last 12 years as a communication and leadership trainer and speaker.

While my work takes me Australia-wide, home is in the Gippsland region of south-east Victoria. As a region, Gippsland has experienced great change over the last 30 years, most significantly in the aftermath of State Electricity Commission (SEC) privatisation by the conservative state government in the 1990s.

I've seen what happens when change occurs in the absence of courageous, supportive, people-focussed leadership. I have seen the impact of industry privatisation, factory closures, lack of investment and major transition on the mindset, sense of self-worth, mental and physical health of a community when it's not handled well, and I don't want to see that happen again.

As I write this book, Gippsland is in the midst of another huge transition as Australia and the world shift to a cleaner energy future that is seeing our region's coal-fired power stations and mines closing. On top of that, we've got a timber industry in transition after the government's decision to stop logging native forests. Add in the global pressures of climate change, the COVID-19 pandemic and the rising cost of living and you've got a region grappling to reinvent itself again for a positive future.

Gippsland is not alone in its challenges. Enormous change is happening worldwide on both a macro and micro scale. That is why I've written this book. To equip you as a leader with the skills to steer through the storm.

Steer Through the Storm is my second book for leaders and a companion to my first book, Soft is the New Hard: How to Communicate Effectively Under Pressure. While you don't have to have read one to benefit from the other, the two go together well. Soft is the New Hard influenced positive change in the behaviour and communication of many leaders around the world. My hope is that Steer Through the Storm does the same with my trademark practical, relatable, plain-speak style. I'm not going to try to impress you with big words, complex theories, dry facts and figures. I'm going to use stories, simple strategies and actionable advice to equip you with the skills you need to succeed.

Sceptical? Good. Sceptics are my favourite people to work with. This book busts the old management myth that you can simply steamroll your people through change and get transformational results. Instead, it makes the case for leading in a way that people want to follow.

But don't make the mistake of thinking that then means this book is soft and fluffy, or that the so-called "soft" skills taught in it are easy. Hell, they're the hardest part. That's why my first book was called *Soft is the New Hard*. This is tough stuff and you can't shirk away from it. The "people bit" is the hardest part of leadership.

Taking the approach to leadership outlined in this book – steering rather than steamrolling or shirking – is not just about being a good human (although that's not a bad thing), it's about steering through change in a way that gets results. It's about making your leadership more effective during the toughest times and ultimately making your job easier.

HOW TO USE THIS BOOK

I've written this book to be read from start to finish, and also to be easy to dip in and out of because I know that as a leader navigating change, you're busy. That's why there are lots of subheadings, highlighted reflection prompts and actions, dot points with questions and tips, and scripts that you can use immediately.

I want this to be a book you come back to again and again. Read it through in full first and then use it as an ongoing resource and guidebook.

But before you read any further, I want to offer you an important piece of advice: do not try to implement all the strategies in this book at once. Improving your leadership through change is a big project, so start small and remember that developing a new skill takes time. As you would with any big project, break the implementation of the strategies in this book down into small, manageable chunks and then break them down further into tangible actions that are specific to you, your development and circumstance. Pick one or two things to focus on initially, get conscious of them, make a commitment to practicing them, and hold yourself accountable for doing them. Once you've got those strategies bedded down, look at adding more in. Skill stack your way to success.

If some of the principles that underpin this book are already familiar to you, the question I want you to ponder as you read on is this: *if I know it, am I doing it?* If you know these strategies, are you implementing them as you lead yourself and your people through change? Because knowing and doing are two very different things and it's the doing that matters. There's no point talking the talk if you're not walking the walk.

PART 1

WHY

Chapter 1

LEADING THROUGH CHANGE

Brad felt like he was out of control. The decision to restructure the unit wasn't his idea but as a team leader, he had responsibility for implementing it. And it did not go well. His people were angry and resistant, declaring the change a stupid idea and waste of time. His upper management were frustrated and impatient, pushing Brad to do more to get his people on board. And then there was Brad, caught in the middle with no idea what he was meant to do or how he was meant to lead his people through.

As he attempted to placate both groups, Brad felt like he was losing the trust and respect of both. The constant bitching, bickering and stonewalling was dragging him down and he didn't know how to get things back on track.

He wanted to throw his hands in the air and shout "What the hell am I meant to do here?"

If only he knew the answer.

Change is challenging and uncertainty is unnerving. It sends many people into a spiral that is hard to deal with as a leader. Your team may get bogged down in gossip, rumour and conspiracy theories. They can become resistant, angry, upset and distracted. That leads to you getting frustrated and your tolerance slipping. You may feel completely out of your depth and wish you could simply deliver the change message, have it accepted and implemented, and then move on. If only it were that simple. But it's not. "Just get on with it" doesn't work when you're dealing with the emotional beings that are humans.

MORE HEART, LESS HEAD

Leading THROUGH change is different to leading change but it's just as important. It's not leading the overall change itself (deciding what the change is and leading its implementation), or managing the change (systems, structures, processes). Leading through change is about supporting your team through the rough seas so they make it through in the best shape possible. More heart, less head. Even if you can't control the change, you don't like it, and there's no "win" for your people, you have a responsibility as a leader to guide your people through.

That's not to say that the project management processes of navigating change are not important. They are! You do often need systems, structures, processes, coalitions and working groups to make change happen well. This "head" stuff is important. But the "heart" – the leading emotion-driven people bit – is too often overlooked. You need a combination of both. There are hundreds, if not thousands of books out there on managing change, leading restructures and getting people "on the bus". I'll leave the project and process aspects of change management to them. This book is about the people bit.

Why is that important? Because organisations don't change, people do.

You can have all the processes you like, you can mandate a new way of doing something, you can change the org chart to reflect your restructure, but unless you can get your people to change, the change you're implementing will never succeed.

Simon was a leader in the power industry who found himself responsible for implementing an unpopular change to rosters in his team. Roster changes are notoriously difficult to get across the line and are often met with huge anger and resistance. This case was no different. Despite the fact that Simon didn't come up with the change (that was Simon's management), he was the one who had to deliver the message to his team and ensure it was implemented.

Only he didn't know how.

"I'm just the coordinator," Simon told me when I spoke to him about leading his teammates through the change. "What can I do? It's not my change. I don't like it either. I'm not sure what role I have to play in all of this aside from telling the crew we have to follow the new rosters."

Simon had never been taught how to lead through change. Like many leaders in the industry, he'd been promoted off the back of his technical skills and experience – not his people skills. While Simon had worked hard to develop his leadership over the years, when it came to leading his people through this high-conflict, high-resistance change, he was at a loss to know how to handle it.

His people knew it and took advantage. Simon's pre-start meetings quickly turned into aggressive free-for-alls where people demanded answers and point-blank refused to go onto the new rosters.

Brad and Simon's stories are not uncommon. Many leaders find themselves in a similar position. They don't have the skill or experience to lead change, and sometimes they don't even have the inclination. They've been instructed from above, which makes them feel like they are just the messenger. In these instances it can be tempting to pass the buck of responsibility onto others, but avoiding the elephant doesn't do anyone any favours, least of all you. You are not just the messenger. You are a leader.

That's why the sub-heading of this book is "how to communicate and lead COURAGEOUSLY through change". This stuff isn't easy. Dealing with the feelings of your people when they're angry, scared and resistant is not for the faint-hearted. It takes guts. Nor is it for those who think they can strong-arm their way to people's compliance. It needs a balance of warmth and strength, curiosity and clarity, compassion and challenge, commitment and consistency.

"But Leah, I'm not a counsellor or psychologist!" you might claim. That's ok, I'm not either.

You don't have to be a counsellor or psychologist to lead courageously through change. What you do need to be is human. You need to draw on your humanity to help people through.

The framework I teach you in this book will give you the foundations to be able to communicate and lead yourself and others courageously through any change, big or small, in your personal and professional life. While it's not the be-all-and-end-all (there's no silver bullet answer), the framework will give you the tools to manage the wide range of responses and emotions that change often sparks. Responses that have the potential to create significant challenges for your team or organisation – even if you manage the actual change process well.

Why am I so confident in that? Why do I know the strategies in this book work? Because over the last two years I have trained hundreds of leaders in this model as they face changes in their industries and teams, from closure, to restructures, to government funding cuts and system overhauls. I've also used this model myself to lead through significant challenges and change in my personal life. I've walked the walk, talked the talk and bought the t-shirt. And now I want to share those skills with you.

THE FIVE Cs OF COMMUNICATING AND LEADING COURAGEOUSLY THROUGH CHANGE

This book is jam-packed with practical strategies for courageous communication and leadership through change but to make it easier for you, I've summarised the key elements in a simple and foundational model: five concepts, made up of 10 C-words that flow in a continuous cyclical model. As such, it's best represented as a circle. It never stops and is not strictly one after the other, although on first go, the order is right. After that first lap around the ring, all five elements should be key features in your change leadership approach. That's why I've called them the Five Cs® of Leading Courageously Through Change.

The Five Cs

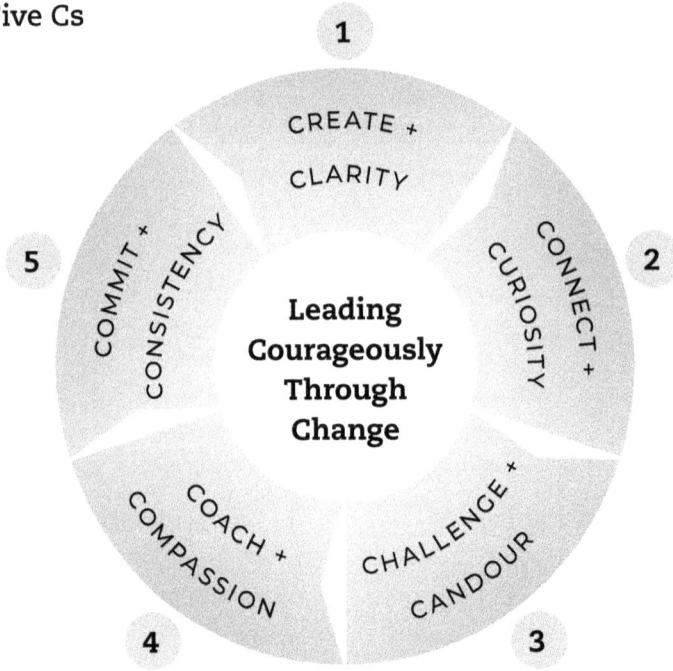

Below I've given you a brief outline of each of the five elements so you have an overview of the entire model before we deep-dive into each step in the second half of this book.

CREATE CLARITY

Create clarity for yourself and your team. Get clear on how you want to navigate the change personally and as a group, clarify your key messages, and then provide that clarity to your team, explaining why the change is needed and why it's important to get through it well.

Even if you don't have all the answers about what the change is or how it affects your people, you can still create a level of clarity by being proactive, clear, concise and transparent in your communication.

CONNECT WITH CURIOSITY

Once you have created clarity, you need to connect with your people, show them you care, and get curious about their feelings and response to the change. Curiosity is an underutilised leadership superpower. It's about asking more questions rather than telling people what to do.

This empathetic approach builds trust and gives you a much greater understanding of where your team is at. You can then use this understanding to lead them much more effectively through the tough times.

CHALLENGE WITH CANDOUR

After you've taken the time to create clarity and connect with curiosity, it's time to challenge the mindsets, focus and response of your people towards the change.

It's only when you have built trust with warmth first that you can challenge your people in a candid and frank way and hold them accountable for their behaviour and performance.

COACH WITH COMPASSION

This is where 1:1 conversations with your staff and your influencing skills come into their own. Coaching conversations empower your people to find their own solutions amidst the storm of change and compassion ensures they feel cared for and supported along the way.

COMMIT WITH CONSISTENCY

Leading through change is not something you do once. It's not one conversation, one meeting or message. It's a process that requires commitment and consistency, repetition and reinforcement.

Many changes fail because they are over-managed and under-communicated. Change leadership and messages need to be instilled into day-to-day activities in new and varied ways.

LEAD YOURSELF FIRST

It starts with you. To be able to lead other people courageously through change, you have to lead yourself first. This was a key message in my first book, *Soft is the New Hard*, and it's where we need to start here as well. Leading your team through change requires an inside-out approach. In most cases, if a change affects your team, it affects you too.

Your emotions and behaviour are contagious. If you don't model the behaviour you want to see in others, how can you expect them to behave in a different way? This means you have to manage your own mindset, emotions and behaviour.

You need to focus on how you respond to challenges, even when you can't change them. And crucially, you must make sure you're looking after yourself with the basics of getting enough sleep, fuelling and moving your body well, and managing your stress levels.

Throughout this book we'll look at how the strategies apply to leading yourself as well as leading others through change.

LEADERSHIP IS ABOUT PEOPLE; MANAGEMENT IS ABOUT TASKS

Let's pause here for a moment to make a distinction between leadership and management. The two words are often used interchangeably but there is a significant difference between them that many people in leadership positions have never been taught.

I'm not talking about the titles within a hierarchy – different organisations do different things in that space. In some workplaces the "Manager" title ranks higher than "Leader" and in other organisations this is reversed.

What I am talking about is the different skill sets required for each. It's not that one is better than the other, it's that they are very different. This book is deliberately and clearly focussed on the leadership space, not management for a reason.

Leadership is about people.
Management is about tasks.

Managers focus on getting the job done – on systems, processes and schedules. A manager oversees a team, instructs people what to do, and plans the next steps. They tell more than they ask and rely on hierarchy and position to get people to do what they need.

Leaders focus on people. They empower a team by engaging people's hearts and minds, they ask questions, model the behaviour they want to see in others, and influence based on trust. A leader is someone people want to follow.

This book is about leadership and as Winston Churchill said: "The difference between mere management and leadership is communication."

Manager v. leader: What's the difference?

Manager	Leader
Focusses on tasks	Focusses on people
Oversees a team	Empowers a team
Focusses on doing things right	Focusses on doing the right thing
Plans and organises	Motivates and develops
Instructs and directs	Coaches and models the behaviour
Relies on hierarchy/position to get people to follow them	Builds trust so people want to follow
Follows the rules	Lives the values
Tells	Asks

©Leah Mether

It's crucial you understand the difference between leadership and management to ensure you bring both skill sets to the table while navigating change. When you're stressed yourself, it's easy to default into management. Systems, processes and plans are practical, logical and give us a sense of control and comfort when our sense of certainty is threatened.

Leadership takes courage. It's messy because humans are messy. There's no one-size-fits-all answer when you're dealing with people.

YOU DON'T HAVE TO LIKE THE CHANGE TO LEAD PEOPLE THROUGH IT

Sometimes you have to lead people through a change you didn't instigate and that you don't like. It may have been imposed on you by executives, a board or a government. In extreme cases as 2020 showed us, it can be a global change no one has any control over, like a pandemic. You might be as resistant to the change as your team. That doesn't mean that you can't lead your people through it.

This is where you have to separate your own feelings about the change from your responsibility as a leader.

You're allowed to be frustrated because the change is poor or it wasn't your idea. That's completely understandable. But when the change is difficult or unpopular, that's when it's most important for you to step up. This is when you really do need to "steer through the storm". It's when you have to make a choice about who you are as a leader.

This is the situation facing leaders in the brown coal power industry in the Latrobe Valley as I write this book. With power station closures slated for the next five to 15 years as the transition away from fossil fuels continues, 1,000+ people will be out of a job. And that change is happening whether people like it or not.

While leaders can't change the closure decisions, they can choose how they respond. They can choose to lead their people well right up until the end, ensuring they retain staff, keep the plants operating, and employ as many people for as long as possible. They can choose to instill pride in their team for powering Victorian homes for more than 50 years, and see out these last few years with a sense of accomplishment at being part of history, much like leaders at Holden did when the Australian car manufacturer stopped production of its cars in Adelaide in 2017.

That doesn't mean you can't express your feelings about the change. But you need to do that in the appropriate forum – up the chain.

The time to argue your case and put forward your opinions is behind closed doors with your bosses. Not in front of your people. In front of them, you need to own the message.

Many leaders think that if they're not on board with a change they don't have a leadership role. Some abdicate responsibility and become absent. Others undermine the change by bitching and whingeing about it in front of the team at every opportunity. Either reaction does huge damage. By stepping back and letting 'it' hit the fan, you're leaving your team at the mercy of those driving the change, who may not have their best interests at heart like you do.

When unpopular or difficult change happens, your people are looking for a leader more than ever. And how you show up will be what they remember. Lead through change well and you will build great trust with your team. Be absent or shirk responsibility and people will lose respect for you and your authority.

REFLECTION

Think about the leaders you most admire. The leaders who have stepped up at times of great change, emergency or crisis. Either leaders you've worked for yourself, or famous leaders you've watched from afar.

Ask yourself:

▸ What did they do that made me see them as a good leader?

▸ What traits did they display?

▸ How did they communicate and behave?

And on the flipside, think of those leaders you've seen in action who have crumbled under pressure. Who have been bullish in their approach or absent at the time of need.

Ask yourself:

▸ What did they do that made me see them as a poor leader through change?

▸ What traits did they display?

▸ How did they communicate and behave?

ANYONE CAN LEAD THROUGH CHANGE

You don't have to be the CEO or leader of the change itself to lead your people through change. Leadership is not a title or position. It's an action and behaviour. You can be a coordinator or supervisor, have no direct reports at all, or simply be a member of a team, and still lead yourself and those around you through change.

Knowing that you can lead without a title or a position of high power in a hierarchy can give you a sense of purpose during great upheaval. Regardless of who you are, you can just do it.

Rachel's husband's family-owned business was under pressure when regulation changes in the logging industry meant new safety management systems had to be implemented.

The changes weren't optional. Either they implemented new safe work procedures and practices, and the logging crew filled out the required paperwork for each job, or they wouldn't be able to continue working.

But the workers were resistant. After all, they'd always done it the old way, without the need for all this extra "fluff and paperwork". Some were disgruntled and annoyed at what they thought was bureaucratic interference in their industry, and fired up whenever the changes were mentioned.

Rachel, who was a stay-at-home mum to two young children at the time, had strong working relationships with members of the logging crew. Overwhelmed by the scale of the changes, her father-in-law and husband pleaded with her to take on the role of OHS representative to implement the systems. She accepted, knowing that their default command-and-control style of demanding compliance wouldn't work.

"Their style was to just lecture, not listen, not care about what the staff said, and to punish anyone who didn't do what they were told.

"I know you catch more flies with honey than you do with vinegar, so I agreed to take on the development and implementation of the safety management system. My husband and his parents were relieved – they didn't really want anything to do with it."

Rachel's approach was very different.

"I used humour, friendliness and grace, coupled with clear, simple language," Rachel explained. "I got up at toolbox meetings and explained why adopting the changes was necessary – if we didn't do it, we'd have no work and we'd lose our contract with the Australian Paper Mill. I explained that this was a change being applied to the entire industry, not just us, and all our competitors were in the same situation too.

"There was a bit of eye rolling to begin with, but I listened to their frustrations and empathised with their concerns. I also encouraged questions. If I couldn't answer them in the moment I'd say, 'Leave that with me,' and I'd follow it up for them. Because I was open, they knew they could trust me. I was approachable and relatable, and balanced being gentle with holding them all to account. The guys could see I was caring and also competent. Finally, after all of that initial resistance, they complied."

The company's safety systems were audited twice within the next nine months. The first audit found 97.5% compliance, and the second 99%.

"I was really proud that we achieved such a fabulous result and I shared the audit results and celebrated these wins with the crews. Because they took up the new procedures so well we were also able to secure an extended contract with Australian Paper Mill, which meant they had secured their jobs. It was a great outcome for everyone."

THE STRONGER YOUR RELATIONSHIPS, THE EASIER IT IS TO LEAD YOUR PEOPLE THROUGH CHANGE

Success is in the set-up. Ideally, you will have built trust with your team and equipped your people with the skills to be adaptive and resilient well before a change happens. If you don't have a positive culture, leading effectively through change is still possible, but it will be much harder.

To increase your influence as a leader through change:

- ▸ Invest time in building relationships of trust with your team.
- ▸ Show your people you care.
- ▸ Take an interest in them as a human, not just a worker.
- ▸ Show your own humanity as a leader.
- ▸ Create open channels of communication.
- ▸ Encourage people to speak up and ask questions.
- ▸ Create an environment of psychological safety where it is safe to speak up.
- ▸ Share information openly when you can.
- ▸ Discuss shared expectations for behaviour.
- ▸ Catch up with your team members for regular one-on-one conversations.
- ▸ Recognise and appreciate people's efforts.

These things may sound basic – and they are – but I am constantly surprised by how many leaders neglect the basics of building a positive team culture and strong relationships, and are then surprised when they find leading through change harder than they expected it to be.

As author Dr Erika James said on the *Dare to Lead* podcast: "If you wait until you need something from your people or team, if you haven't done the pre-work to build trusting relationships, what on earth makes you think they'll be there in your time of need? But if you've done that work in advance, most times people will walk through fire to help you."

You can, and should, lay the foundations
for leading your people courageously
through change now by working on
the culture, trust, communication and
behavioural expectations within your team.

See building and strengthening relationships as essential to your
success, not as a "nice to have" optional extra.

SUMMARY

In this chapter I have outlined the difference between leading
through change and leading change, as well as the difference
between leadership and management.

You now understand that steering others through the storm
requires leading yourself first, and that you don't have to like a
change or be in a senior leadership role to lead your people through
change.

You also appreciate the importance of building relationships and a
positive culture for making your job easier.

But what happens if you don't step up and lead your people
through change? What if you do resort to old-school management
techniques and ignore the feelings of your team? What impact and
cost does that have?

How are your people likely to respond? You'll find out in the next
chapter.

Chapter 2

CAN'T THEY JUST GET ON WITH IT?

"I don't have time for this and I don't do feelings," Graeme, a leader in the water industry told me as we discussed an upcoming change in his team.

Graeme was frustrated that his people were distracted by the uncertainty the change was creating. "I just need them to focus on work, get the job done, and not get caught up in worrying about what they think is and isn't going to happen," he said.

Graeme's response is not an isolated one. I've heard a version of this many times over the years, including from Melanie, a nurse unit manager in a large hospital.

"There should be no such thing as emotion in the workplace," she said, deadpan. "If you have to deliver a hard message, stick to the facts and keep emotions out of it."

That approach might work if only humans were not emotion-driven beings.

Whether you like it or not, emotions underpin and drive human behaviour. We like to think we're rational beings who make rational decisions but we're not, and the more we try to ignore or suppress our emotions, the worse the outcomes often are.

But I get it. As leaders, supporting your people through change can feel relentless. It is exhausting. It can be frustrating.

Sometimes you don't feel like you're leading at all, rather you feel like you're dragging, pushing, pulling, cajoling and fighting tantruming toddlers. Or perhaps you feel like you're stuck in one of those nightmares where you're trying to move forward but your legs don't work and you're either stuck or being pulled backwards.

Leading through change IS hard and it can be tempting to just shout, "Bad luck! We just have to get on with it. Suck it up." But while that might feel good in the moment, the simple fact is – it doesn't work. People can't simply ignore their emotions, fears and concerns, so as their leader you can't either.

CHANGE IS CHALLENGING

There is no change without discomfort. Our brain is wired for comfort and certainty. We like routine, patterns, habits and shortcuts. Reacting to change with caution, apprehension and defensiveness is our normal protection mechanism to any perceived threat.

Understanding the basic neuroscience of how and why we react to and resist change can help us understand how to deal with it. The amygdala – the primitive reptilian part of our brain – interprets change as a threat to our safety and control, and puts us into fight, flight or freeze mode. Even small or positive change can send us off on a spiral – often when we least expect it.

In my workshops, I ask leaders to think about a time when they've been surprised by their own reaction, or that of their team, to a small or positive change. The relatively small changes they've described include things like a microwave or TV being taken from a brew room, desks being moved in an office, hard copy newsletters being replaced with electronic noticeboards, and hot desking instead of having a set desk (although many would argue this is big change). Positive changes that sparked unexpected responses included marriage, new babies, job promotions, moving house, moving in with a partner, separating from a partner, and even divorce. One leader told me how she had been surprised by her feelings after ending an unhappy marriage. "I was relieved and happy to finally be out of it and knew it was absolutely the right call, but I was still hit with fear and grief after the separation that caught me completely off guard," she said. "At first I couldn't understand it but then I realised it was because the change, although positive, brought with it uncertainty."

Although humans are actually highly adaptive and good at adjusting to change over time or when we have to (hello evolution and our response to the COVID pandemic), there are some basic needs we cling to that change can threaten.

These needs were highlighted in my work with leaders at a Latrobe Valley power station that had been given a closure date of 2028. My role was to run initial training to help them understand the impacts of change on themselves and their people, and teach them the foundations to steer their people through the storm of what was set to be a long transition.

In those sessions, we discussed how change can impact our basic human needs, using Maslow's famous Hierarchy of Needs, illustrated below, to identify how big an impact the change was likely to have on people.

SELF-ACTUALISATION
desire to become the most that one can be

ESTEEM
respect, self-esteem, status, recognition, strength, freedom

LOVE AND BELONGING
friendship, intimacy, family, sense of connection

SAFETY NEEDS
personal security, employment, resources, health, property

PHYSIOLOGICAL NEEDS
air, water, food, shelter, sleep, clothing, reproduction

Maslow's Hierachy of Needs

We didn't get very far. For there, on the second rung, *Safety*, was employment, resources, personal security and property. For some people, the loss of their job would threaten this basic need for safety. They were worried whether they would find work post-closure and if they did, whether it would pay anywhere near what their current jobs did. They were worried about the big mortgage they had on their homes, their children's education, the cost of living and their family's future.

The way the hierarchy works, from bottom to top, is that once you hit the level at which your needs are threatened, you can't go any further. So, for those employees who felt their *Safety* needs were unsteady, this is where they were stuck.

The next rung above *Safety* is *Love and Belonging*. This basic need could be threatened for employees with the closure. Some people had worked at the site for their entire 30 or 40 year career. Their colleagues were like family and they couldn't comprehend a life without the daily connection with work friends.

Above that is *Esteem*. Those at the power station who were confident of finding future employment and not worried about losing their basic *Safety* needs could get wobbly at the *Esteem* rung. There is status, recognition, respect and freedom in working a power station job in the Latrobe Valley. The jobs are incredibly well paid and competition to get them is fierce. The loss of this job for some may threaten their sense of *Esteem*.

Talking through the basic needs we have as humans opened the leaders' eyes to the significance of the change they were facing. They knew it was big and would have a massive impact, but to see these basic human needs outlined brought the magnitude home.

REFLECTION

1 . Consider your own reactions to changes you've experienced in your life. Even positive changes you instigated. How did you react? How did you feel leading up to the change? What emotions and anxieties did you experience?

2. Consider a change facing you or your team. Which rung on Maslow's Hierarchy of Needs does it influence, impact or threaten?

RESISTANCE IS REAL AND HAS REASONS

It's easy to dismiss those who resist change as just choosing to be difficult, particularly if they're in a well-paid job with good conditions. And sure, occasionally that's true. But in most cases, once you get past the initial fight, flight or freeze response, you'll see that people resist change for a reason.

In her fantastic book *Transforming Norm: Leading the Change to a Mentally Healthy Workforce*, Tanya Heaney-Voogt outlines eight reasons people resist change. I've added a ninth.

They are:

1. They disagree there is a need for change.
2. They agree on the need for change but not on the solution.
3. They resist the sender of the message.
4. They are uncertain of the implications of the change and what it means for them.
5. They fear loss.
6. They resist because they can, it's "fun", and they're jaded.
7. They were told, not consulted.
8. They have change fatigue or work overload and don't feel they have capacity to take on anything else.
9. They have experienced poor change before and don't trust that it will be done differently this time.

One of these reasons is enough for people to rebel against a change, but if you hit on multiple points because your change has been poorly communicated and led, expect high emotion and potential conflict.

At the secondary school where Emily worked, the principal dropped news on the last day of a stressful term that all staff had to move staffrooms that day. She gave no explanation of why or what for. This meant staff had to shift all their possessions, resources, desks and furniture before the early finish at 1:30pm.

"She just dropped the bomb at the morning all-staff meeting and was then surprised that it blew up in her face. She announced the news at the very end of the meeting with no discussion or question time available, and then got annoyed that staff were upset later that day. She genuinely couldn't see what she'd done wrong," Emily said.

The principal's bulldozer approach gave staff reasons 2, 3, 7 and 8 on the list.

Understanding why people are resistant to a particular change will help you to be able to lead them through it and determine the messaging that will best resonate.

For example:

Reason people resist change	What to do about it
1. They disagree there is a need for change.	You need to go harder on the "why" part of your message.
2. They agree on the need for change but not on the solution.	In addition to explaining why the change is needed, you also need to make clear what other options were considered and why this one was landed on.
3. They resist the sender of the message.	You need to focus on building trust with your people, whether you are the sender or someone else is.
4. They are uncertain of the implications of the change and what it means for them.	You need to create more clarity for your team about the who, what, when, where, why and how of the change (see Chapter 5).
5. They fear loss.	This is often valid, particularly if the change relates in a tangible loss for them. In this case you need to deal with the feelings of your people, empathise and support them through their emotional response.
6. They resist because they can, it's "fun", and they're jaded.	This is a real challenge. In these circumstances, setting clear expectations for behaviour and holding people to account is vital. Be careful about giving too much time to the haters (see Chapter 7).
7. They were told, not consulted.	Communicate early and often. If they were not consulted for a reason, explain why.
8. They have change fatigue or work overload.	Reset priorities in the team and do what you can to clear the decks and create space. Cut or delay anything that is a "nice to do" rather than "have to do" right now. Beware of bundling too many unrelated changes together.

9.	They have experienced poor change before and don't trust that it will be done differently this time.	Acknowledge the failures of the past, the learnings you've taken, and explain how it will be different this time.

Not sure why your people are resisting? Don't be afraid to ask them outright. Their response may give you valuable insight and you may then be able to involve them in resolving the concerns.

Command and control should be a last resort

"What if they're not on board?" Sally asked her boss in their leadership meeting to discuss new reporting lines being introduced across her organisation. "I can see there being a lot of resistance to these changes." Sally knew she was going to have a hard time convincing her 10 staff members that a split in reporting lines within the team was a good idea. In fact, she knew they would hate it.

Sally's manager, a man in his mid-50s who was used to getting his own way without questions asked, hiked his eyebrows, looked at Sally incredulously and said: "If they don't like it, they can leave."

Sally recounted this story to me later with a shake of her head. "Never mind there's a massive skills shortage, these guys are good workers, they've been with us for years, and just getting people to apply for government jobs is a challenge because of the lower wages we can offer...His answer to dealing with people who don't like the change is to tell them to leave. If I do that I'll end up with no staff!"

Sadly, this old-school command and control dictatorial style of management still exists.

Forcing change with a steamroller approach can feel fast and effective but it will cost you dearly and can have significant unintended consequences such as:

- high turnover of staff
- people off on sick and stress leave
- HR complaints
- poor culture
- low morale
- high conflict
- safety failures
- low productivity.

It may also come at a high personal cost. Battling against a resistant team is a killer for your stress levels and mental health. You feel like you're going to war rather than work and are always on high alert waiting for the next attack, gotcha moment or booby trap. You don't sleep, your tolerance is shot, and you're probably not much fun to be around – at work or at home.

It can be tempting though – particularly if there is resistance to the change – because emotions are tricky and you just want to get the job done. You're frustrated, time poor and probably also being pressured by above to implement the change and get results. But as Brent Gleeson and Mark Owen write in their book *TakingPoint: A Navy SEAL's 10 Fail Safe Principles for Leading Through Change*, "…most organisational change efforts fail because they happen in overmanaged, under-led command-and-control environments."

Strongarming change with a "tell" approach without dealing with the legitimate concerns, questions and feelings of your people will not get you the results you need. Sure, at a surface level it might look like you've had success. The structure might have changed on paper and the reporting lines are technically different. But if

Sally and her boss didn't explain the reasons behind the decision and listen to the worries of staff, the change was unlikely to be successful. People find ways to work around changes that are forced upon them like this. Those workarounds can be well intentioned to make the best of it, or they can be a form of white anting, of undermining the change because they didn't want it or didn't feel listened to in the first place.

People don't like being told what to do and when they are, they resist. That doesn't mean there aren't times when a more forceful "tell" approach is required. Consider emergency responses or the restrictions and mandates implemented during the height of the COVID pandemic. In those situations, you do sometimes need to command and control to respond quickly and keep people safe. But even in the midst of a crisis, you can still empathise.

AVOIDANCE MAKES PROBLEMS GROW

While a command and control "tell" approach should be a last resort when leading through change, avoiding leadership all together by sticking your head in the sand and pretending the change is not happening can be even more damaging. When you avoid the elephant in the room, or shirk your responsibility as a people leader by leaving it up to others to be the messenger, the problems don't magically disappear. In fact, they often grow in size. What starts out as a few quiet rumblings and niggles about the impending change can quickly escalate into whopping great issues that are even harder to deal with as the emotion is heightened.

So why do some leaders, particularly those who did not instigate the change, avoid taking an active role in leading their people through it? Here are my top three reasons:

1. They don't see it as their role.

It's not their change so why get involved any more than they have to? These "leaders" don't understand the difference between leadership and management. They figure they're not a psychologist or counsellor so dealing with the emotions of people is surely outside their remit.

2. They don't know how to do it.

They don't feel they have the skills to have the hard conversations under pressure or deal with the feelings that are coming up for their people. They don't know where to start and are struggling to process their own emotions let alone someone else's – so they do nothing and pretend like the problem doesn't exist.

3. They don't want to do it.

Afterall, it's not their change. Why stick your own neck out and risk getting your team offside if you don't have to? Surely it's better to stay quiet and let others sort it out (or stuff it up).

I get it. Sometimes it's tempting to shirk responsibility for delivering a difficult change message or dealing with the complex people part of leadership. You just want your people to turn up, leave life at home and get the job done. But avoiding dealing with the feelings of your people or suppressing your own is not healthy and will not end well. While someone may be able to keep their fear, anger and frustration at bay for a little while, that pent up feeling has to go somewhere and often explodes spectacularly. You end up with an even bigger problem than you would have faced if you'd had the courage to deal with and work through people's emotions head on.

The other consequence of avoidance is losing the trust and respect of your people. If your people feel like you don't care about them (apathy) or that you've just thrown your hands in the air, given up and are avoiding dealing with the hard conversations, they are likely to give up as well.

Consider your natural approach to leading through change. Be honest. Are you more of a steamroller, steerer or shirker?

Steamroller

- Is high energy.
- Gets the job done.
- Is all about action.
- Steamrolls through resistance.
- Is fast and forward focussed.
- Does more telling than asking.
- Uses command and control.
- Leaves people behind.

Steerer

- Asks more questions.
- Takes a considered approach.
- Gets curious about where they're going and how to bring others along.
- Steers people in a positive direction with influence based on trust.
- Looks at options.
- Has a vision for where they're going and where they want to be, but is open to different ways of getting there.
- Holds people accountable for behaviour.

Shirker

- ▸ Avoids dealing with the change and having conversations.
- ▸ Waits for someone else to take the lead.
- ▸ Doesn't take personal responsibility for their own leadership role.
- ▸ Puts their head in the sand.
- ▸ Expects the change to just magically happen and for them and the team to be swept along in the current.
- ▸ Is surprised when people react to change negatively or with resistance.

Recognising that you can be a steamroller or a shirker doesn't make you a bad person or even necessarily a poor leader. The fact that you acknowledge it means you can do something about it.

ORGANISATIONS DON'T CHANGE, PEOPLE DO

In their book *TakingPoint*, Brent Gleeson and Mark Owen wrote: "In any transformation, mindsets and behaviours must first change in order for the culture to begin shifting in the needed direction."

Organisational change won't stick unless your people change.

Even if you change processes, structure, policies and tasks within your business, if your people are not on board they will revert to their old habits. If you don't slow down, get your messaging right and engage with your people first, they'll fall back on what they know.

This is important to understand as sometimes, in the frustration of wanting to make a change quickly, it can be tempting to jump over the slower process of engaging staff and simply make the change with the hope that they'll eventually come around. While this approach might be necessary in emergency situations, it should not be a default strategy.

When you try to push a change through too fast, without bringing your people along with it, you'll actually slow down the process rather than speed it up, because implementation and acceptance will be slower.

Investing the time upfront will almost always save you time by minimising resistance and people problems later on.

Let me put my own hand up and make a confession: I'm crap at slowing down. I'm a high-action, "get the job done" person, possibly like you. I'm as tempted to skip over this part as you are. But that would be skipping vital information. You see, being a high-action leader will help you in many ways throughout your career, but in this context it can hold you back. You might personally adapt to the change and lead yourself through it, but when you look over your shoulder to check that your team is with you, they'll be nowhere to be seen.

I see this play out frequently in well-meaning organisations with good intentions, such as organisations where leaders are trying to change embedded toxic cultures or get rid of gender bias and increase diversity. These are wonderful changes to strive for, but changing the organisation's hiring practices on their own, without working on shifting the mindsets, attitudes and beliefs of your people, risks the change being tokenistic, and in some cases even dangerous. Imagine being a young female, hired into a male-dominated, blokey-bloke organisation as part of a diversity and inclusion program, only to be bullied, discriminated against and belittled by your colleagues in underhanded ways. How much damage could that well-intentioned action do to the person you're trying to promote? It might sound extreme but I have seen this happen.

Changing systems on their own is not enough. You have to take time to engage with your people and their complex emotions, feelings and beliefs through change if you want it to be successful.

DEALING WITH THE FEELING ISN'T OPTIONAL IF YOU WANT YOUR CHANGE TO BE SUCCESSFUL

In this chapter you have learned not only that your people can't "just get on with it" but that by telling them to do so, or not addressing their emotions and concerns at all, you make things worse.

Simply telling people what to do or avoiding tough conversations at times of change is not leadership. Leadership requires dealing with the feelings of your people and in the next chapter we'll look at what some of those common feelings and responses to change can be.

Chapter 3

DEALING WITH THE FEELING

As Dale Carnegie wrote in his classic book *How to Win Friends and Influence People* way back in 1936: "When dealing with people, let us remember we are not dealing with creatures of logic. We are dealing with creatures of emotion."

We have to deal with the feelings of our people if we want to have any chance of leading them successfully through change.

Now, let me be clear: dealing with the feelings of your people as you steer them through the storm is not about getting everyone in your team into the happy zone and embracing the change with gusto. Expecting people to hold hands and sing 'Kumbaya' with smiles on their faces as they're being made redundant during a restructure is delusional. Some people will be angry, some people will be sad – and that's ok.

Dealing with the feeling is about leading your people to acceptance so they can move through the change in the best way possible, choosing how they respond rather than getting stuck in a negative reaction.

You don't have to be a psychologist, counsellor or emotional intelligence expert to do it. You just have to be human and to connect to the humanity of your people. With a little more knowledge about how emotions and feelings impact you and others experiencing change, your leadership and ability to handle the varied responses that come at you will improve greatly. There are some common feelings and emotions that arise in response to change and in this chapter I'm going to introduce you to them. Because in many cases, simply acknowledging that these feelings exist can make a big difference.

THE DIFFERENCE BETWEEN EMOTIONS, FEELINGS AND MOODS

Before I get into the common reactions to change, let me start with a quick and dirty explanation of the difference between emotions, feelings and moods.

These terms are often used interchangeably but there are key differences between them and it can be helpful to understand what they are.

According to emotional intelligence expert Sue Langley, CEO and founder of The Langley Group, the difference between the three is as follows.

EMOTIONS

Emotions are linked to our body and our brain. They are physical, quick and occur automatically and instinctively, usually without conscious thought. They can impact and influence attention, thought and behaviour.

There are no "good" or "bad" emotions. Emotions are simply data on what our body and brain are experiencing. Some emotions, our primary emotions, are universal across cultures and have a survival value.

For example, the emotion of fear occurs when we face a possible threat, be it physical or psychological. It triggers a physical response by elevating our heart rate and triggering the amygdala to put us into fight, flight or freeze mode. The emotion of surprise, however, comes when something unexpected happens. It often causes us to gasp. Whereas anger happens when we're blocked from getting something or something is in our way. We often get a surge of energy along with it.

FEELINGS

Feelings are the physiological sensation of emotions, or rather, how an emotion makes you feel. The emotion comes first and is universal. The feeling it produces varies from person to person depending on your experience and personality. Two people can experience the same emotion but feel it very differently.

For example: one of my favourite physical activities to do is obstacle racing. Think Tough Mudder, Spartan Race – anything that involves crawling through mud, swinging off ropes and challenging myself in ways I never would in my normal life. Many of the obstacles scare me. And for me, that's what makes them exciting. The emotion of fear hits, I get that primitive surge of adrenalin in response, and the feeling I experience is one of excitement, which translates into me saying "let's go" and running to be first in line to tackle the task before my self-doubt can kick in and I chicken out. For others the emotion of fear may feel debilitating and mean jumping on a giant swing is the last thing they want to do. They experience the same emotion but feel it differently. In their mind, the feeling of fear is dangerous, which means stop, so they step out of line, walk down from the obstacle and don't try it. The emotion can elicit a different feeling.

MOODS

According to Langley, a mood is more ongoing and less reactive to stimulus, events or changes. For example, you might be tired and grumpy. No matter what happens that day – be it good or bad – your mood may stay dark and your tolerance levels low.

In this book, we'll be investigating emotions, feelings and moods because they all have an impact on you, your people and your leadership during times of change and uncertainty.

EXPECT EMOTION, PREPARE FOR FEELINGS

Feelings and emotions underpin everything that we do. They drive human behaviour – our choices, decisions, performance and actions. We ignore them at our peril.

American academic and author Brené Brown nailed it in her bestselling book *Dare to Lead* when she wrote: "Leaders must either invest a reasonable amount of time attending to fears and feelings, or squander an unreasonable amount of time trying to manage ineffective and unproductive behaviour."

People drive performance but if you don't pay attention to how they feel about change, they'll drive problems instead. The reality is, if we don't invest time and energy in "dealing with the feelings" of our people, it will cost us time, money and productivity in terms of distraction, conflict, disagreements, complaints, stress leave, culture and resignations. If your people flounder, you'll be the one who cops it. Your people will not do their best work, may jump ship completely, or put safety at risk through distraction.

Ignoring the emotions and feelings of your people as they react to change will only see these problems grow, and often the poor behaviour will continue. So expect emotion – in both yourself and others.

Don't be angered or surprised by it. Your people are having a normal human reaction to challenge, uncertainty and change.

That doesn't excuse poor behaviour and you still have to hold your people to account but it is important to consider the context that behaviour sits in.

EQ IS THE NEW IQ

Being able to deal with the feelings and emotions of your people requires a base level of emotional intelligence, a term you have no doubt heard (if not understood) in recent years.

So what is emotional intelligence and why is it worth developing as a leader?

Coined by Jack Mayer and Peter Salovey in 1990, emotional intelligence is essentially your ability to perceive, use, understand and manage emotions in yourself and others.

According to Mayer and Salovey, it's: "The ability to monitor one's own and others' feelings and emotions, to discriminate among them, and to use this information to guide one's thinking and action."

As I wrote in *Soft is the New Hard,* a high EQ is becoming as highly valued as a high IQ in the workplace – for good reason. A person with a high intellectual intelligence is of little use if they can't control their anger and aggression, if they lack self-awareness and they can't work well with or influence others.

Emotionally intelligent people have high self-awareness and adjust their communication to work with the emotions of other people, creating a connection with those around them. They stay calm under pressure and empathise with other people, even if that other person's response is different to their own. That makes them valuable.

Developing your emotional intelligence is one of the most impactful ways to improve your communication, particularly under pressure, and many organisations now hire for it.

If you want to get a solid understanding of where you sit when it comes to emotional intelligence, consider taking a Mayer, Salovey, Caruso Emotional Intelligence Test (MSCEIT) – the only abilities-based test for EQ – and getting a debrief with an accredited practitioner. A Google search will give you a range of options.

COMMON RESPONSES TO CHANGE

The responses people often have to change are similar to the stages of grief – so much so that one of the most famous models of change and its impact on people is the Kubler-Ross Change Curve, which is based on the stages of grief originally developed by Elisabeth Kubler-Ross in her 1969 book *On Death and Dying*, and then built on with co-author David Kessler decades later in the classic book *On Grief and Grieving*.

The Kubler-Ross model is often used to help people understand their reaction to any significant change or upheaval they experience, not just a death or tragedy.

The five stages identified in Kubler-Ross's original model were: denial, anger, bargaining, depression and acceptance.

In 2020, David Kessler suggested there was a sixth stage in his book *Finding Meaning: The Sixth Stage of Grief,* written after the death of his 21-year-old son. Despite being a grief expert for most of his professional life, Kessler realised there was a missing piece in his work that could help him and others find a way through unexpected and devastating loss. He dubbed this sixth stage of grief "finding meaning".

Although the Kubler-Ross Change Curve was originally represented as a linear curve, with one step following another, it is now widely understood that the stages are not linear at all. Not all people go through all stages, and different people will be at different places at different times. For this reason, I have represented the six stages in a simple box model below, with a brief explanation of each underneath.

It is useful to understand the various common ways people respond to change so you are prepared for what may come and are not unprepared or surprised by the reactions you may see.

Kubler-Ross Stages of grief/responses to change

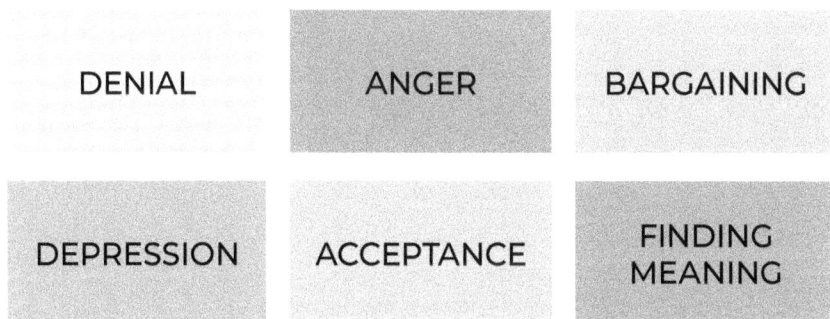

DENIAL	ANGER	BARGAINING
DEPRESSION	ACCEPTANCE	FINDING MEANING

DENIAL

You convince yourself the change is not going to happen or that it won't affect you.

You avoid conversations and communication about the change and pretend everything is normal.

You disengage from change talk and get frustrated when time is spent focussed on the change because "it's never going to happen".

ANGER

You're in pain, you fear loss, and you need someone to blame.

When people are angry they often look for a scapegoat. In this situation it might be the organisation, the leadership team or an individual decision-maker.

Your tolerance is low, communication aggressive and behaviour explosive – sometimes like a tantruming toddler.

In this stage you may also be suspicious, frustrated, resentful, cynical and resistant. You're not open to listening to how the change could benefit you, you argue and express your vocal opposition in front of others.

You possibly even threaten and yell. You may be defiant, refusing to follow instructions or adopt the change.

BARGAINING

In this stage you may try to bargain your way out of the change or endeavour to minimise its impact on you.

This stage can see some people start sucking up to managers to curry favour or improving their performance in the hope of protecting their job. Common phrases are, "If only…" and "What if…"

What if we improve our performance – would that stop us from closing?

What if I hoard all the knowledge I have about this process – would that help me keep my job?

What if we resist and hold out – will that mean the change can't happen?

DEPRESSION

You become sad and despondent in this stage as your grief hits a deeper level.

You may withdraw, disengage, feel a sense of hopelessness, and wonder if it's worth going on through the change at all. "What's the point?" you think.

You may also feel overwhelmed and frozen, becoming more dependent on your boss.

You may also become very quiet and avoid speaking up or contributing at all.

Note: We are not talking about clinical depression as a mental illness here, but a depressive state.

ACCEPTANCE

You accept the change is happening. You don't necessarily like it or agree with it, but you understand that it is what it is and make a choice to live with it.

You stop resisting, bitching and whingeing about it, and move on, adjusting to the change with pragmatism.

When you reach acceptance, you are able to focus on your job, remain calm, and be ok in the middle of the challenge that change brings.

FINDING MEANING

You look for the learnings that came out of the change and find meaning in them.

You don't get hung up on the fact the change happened, rather you become conscious of how you have changed and evolved through the process. You take your learnings into future challenges.

Finding meaning takes time and is relative and personal to each individual.

REFLECTION

1. Think about a big change or loss you have experienced in your professional or personal life. Can you identify the stages of grief that you went through?

2. If you're leading your team through a change right now, consider where the various people in your team are at. Can you identify the stage different people are in at the moment?

THERE'S NO "ONE-SIZE-FITS-ALL" RESPONSE

While it's important for you to expect emotion from your people, and to be aware of the common responses to change, it's also crucial to understand that there is no one-size-fits-all response. People are affected by change in different ways, they respond in different ways, have different histories and past experiences of change, and different communication styles.

As a leader, you must be prepared to adapt and adjust. You need to step back and consider the various ways change may impact your people, and not be surprised if you get a whole gamut of responses within your team.

Let's take a look as some real-life examples of the variety of possible responses. I was working with leaders at an energy generator that was transitioning towards closure in six years' time. I asked the leaders about their people's responses to the closure news and how it differed depending on where a person was at in their career and life.

Here are some of the responses leaders spoke of:

- Some staff asked when the transition program was kicking in because the company should be offering more support by now given it was only six years away.
- Others asked why the transition program was starting now, because closure was still six years away.
- Older workers who would retire after closure saw it as a positive way to close out their careers.
- Workers in their late 40s to early 50s were concerned about whether they would be able to find work again at this late point in their careers.
- Younger leaders saw it as an opportunity to lead through significant change, which would look good on a resume when they went for a new position.
- Some workers wanted to jump ship now and find more "secure" employment elsewhere.
- Others wanted to stay until the end and look at ways to be kept on for rehabilitation works.
- Some people worried about how they would pay their mortgages and whether they would be able to maintain their lifestyle post-closure.
- Some were worried they would have to take a significant pay cut in their next job if they wanted to stay in the local region.
- Some workers were considering fly-in-fly-out work to maintain their lifestyle and level of income.
- Some people felt grateful to have a clear plan and years of notice until closure, unlike a nearby station and mine which closed five months after its announcement.

This list shows how varied the responses to change can be and why, as a leader, you need to be prepared for people to react in different ways. You cannot make assumptions that just because you are comfortable with the change, that your people will be too. Or just because one person is angry, that everyone will be.

THE REACTION DOES NOT NECESSARILY CORRESPOND WITH THE EMOTION UNDERPINNING IT

Be aware – the behaviour and reaction you may see in response to a change may not necessarily correspond with or represent the emotion that underpins it.

This is particularly the case for men. I know that's a generalisation, but stay with me...Much of my work is in male-dominated workplaces with men in traditionally blue-collar roles. In these workplaces, feelings and emotions are not something that are often expressed freely or acknowledged.

Many of these men were raised to believe emotions are bad and expressing them was "only for girls". As a boy, they were meant to be strong, harden up and definitely not cry. When I ask them if there was one emotion they were allowed to express – a "manly" emotion that was safe for them to show without being ridiculed – their answer is immediate and unanimous: anger.

> Many men were raised to believe they had to bottle up all emotion except anger. Anger they could express and so they did (and some still do).

The challenge is, this programming is so engrained for some men that their response to any uncomfortable feeling or emotion is to express it with anger. Feel scared and uncertain? Get angry. Embarrassed and ashamed? Explode with anger to cover it up. Again and again, I see examples of this version of masculinity playing out in poor, aggressive and angry behaviour by (most often but not always) men in the workplace.

It's something to be aware of as you try to unlock what's going on for your people as they navigate uncertainty and change. Although you may be seeing anger, it might be something else entirely that underpins it.

That was certainly the case for Bob.

Bob was in his early 50s and had worked in planning and scheduling for more than 30 years.

Mia was Bob's boss. And she was frustrated.

Mia had introduced a new, more modern process for recording plans and documents. A process that required scanning hard copy forms and filing them electronically in a new software system, rather than using old school filing cabinets.

Bob didn't want a bar of it. His old process worked perfectly fine, thank you very much.

When Mia insisted the new process had to be followed, Bob resisted. And he expressed that resistance with anger.

When Mia spoke to me she was unsure of her next steps. "He is flat out refusing to do it," she said. "Won't even entertain the idea. Just gets angry, refuses and said if it's worked for 30 years, it can work for plenty more. It's getting to the stage where I'm going to have to give him a formal warning or start performance management, which seems ridiculous over such a trivial and simple process change."

As I listened to Mia's frustrations, a question emerged in my mind. "Have you tried showing him the new process rather than telling him about it, or writing it in an email?" I asked.

"Have you walked through the steps with him so he can see what's involved? I'm wondering if his anger might be a cover to disguise his embarrassment that he doesn't know how to use the scanner and he's too proud to admit it or ask for help."

Turns out, I'd guessed right.

Later that very day, Mia tapped Bob on the shoulder and said, "Come with me," and then, without even suggesting he didn't know how to use the scanner, she stepped Bob through the new process, showing him where to put the paper, which buttons to press, and how to then access the files on a computer and store them correctly.

The whole process took her about 15 minutes. And although Bob grumbled his way through it, he finally got it.

The next day he started using the scanner and following the process.

Bob's anger hadn't been because he hated the change at all. It was a cover for his real feeling of inadequacy and being left behind by changes in technology.

A bit of thinking, consideration of the underlying feeling, and adapting her approach to leading Bob through the change, meant Mia finally got the result she was after. Her small investment in time saved her a mountain of further angst continuing to deal with Bob's anger and resistance.

ALLOW YOURSELF TO FEEL

Now, I appreciate that all this talk about emotions and feelings might be making you uncomfortable.

The idea of actually being allowed to feel emotions and acknowledge them may be a new concept for you. A scary concept. If you were raised to believe emotions = weakness, you also probably heard the common catchcries of "don't be a wuss" and "don't get emotional" while you were growing up. Those early messages inform what you do as an adult.

For many of my clients, that leads to severe and often devastating emotional suppression. They bottle up their emotions so tightly, stuff them down and ignore them, or numb out with alcohol, drugs and overwork, to the point where they don't deal with their issues and instead pretend everything is ok.

Until it's not.

And then they explode, get sick, disassociate or self-destruct.

Emotional suppression is not an effective leadership or self-management strategy – for you or your people. The quickest and most courageous way to get through a challenging time is to face up to your feelings and emotions, and then work through them. You've got to allow yourself to feel.

There are no bad emotions. None. As I said earlier and will say again: emotions are data. They give you information about what your body and mind are experiencing.

It's what you do with those emotions, and the actions that you take, that is important.

You need to be able to regulate your emotions so that you can express and process them in an appropriate way. Not suppress them.

You can't blunt one emotion without blunting them all. If you don't allow yourself to feel the hard emotions – like grief, frustration, and sadness – you're unintentionally blunting your ability to experience emotions like joy, love and happiness too.

INCREASE YOUR EMOTIONAL VOCABULARY

If I asked you to describe how you feel about work right now, using two words, what would they be? And "good" is not an answer.

Could you do it? Could you pinpoint the main emotions or feelings you're experiencing?

I often use this question at the start of my workshops to get a read on the room and where people are at. I'm also often surprised by how challenging many people find the activity.

If you want to be able to lead your people through change more effectively, in addition to understanding responses to change, it is important to increase your emotional vocabulary. Most of us aren't very good at getting granular and specific when describing how we feel. In fact, many people can't name more than a handful of emotions when pressed. Happy, sad and angry are the top three, and some struggle to go past that.

It's hard to deal with the feelings and emotions of your people if you can't articulate, or help them articulate, what those feelings and emotions are.

Being able to label the specific emotion you're experiencing allows you to process it more effectively. When you can name it, you can work through it. You are better placed to make sense of what is happening and will be more likely to get to the heart of the issue if you can articulate the feeling that underpins it.

To help you improve your emotional vocabulary, I have included a copy of Geoffrey Roberts's *Emotional Word Wheel*, inspired Dr Gloria Willcox's model *The Feelings Wheel* on the following page. It includes 130 emotion and feeling words. You can download a printable version on the Resources page of my website at www.leahmether. com.au.

I use this wheel to help leaders put words to how they are feeling and support their staff to do the same. A number of my leadership clients also use the wheel in their 1:1 meetings with staff to help them articulate where they're at.

It's particularly helpful if you lead a team of people with limited emotional vocabulary as it gives them words to choose from. Rather than have to wrack their brains for words to sum up the feeling, they can simply point to the wheel. And once they can name it, they and you can address it.

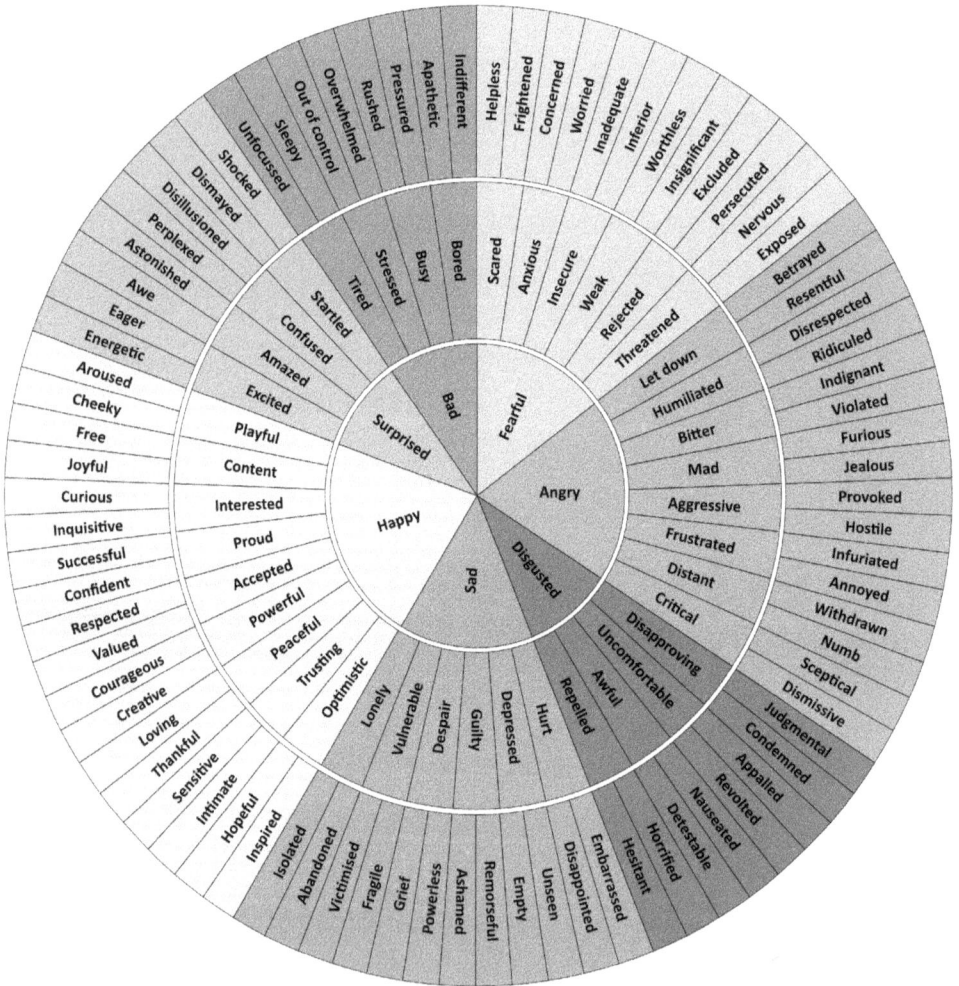

Emotional Word Wheel by Geoffrey Roberts, inspired by Dr Gloria Willcox's The Feeling Wheel

For you:

Looking at the Emotional Word Wheel, how do you feel about work and your leadership at the moment? If you're navigating a professional change, which two words best sum up how you feel and why?

Challenge yourself to get more granular than "happy", "sad", or "angry".

With your team:

Try using the wheel with your staff too. Ask them in their next 1:1, *"If you had to name the main emotion or feeling you've been experiencing at work in the last month, what would it be?"* or *"If you had to choose a word from this wheel to describe how you're feeling about the change at the moment, what would it be?"*

Then get curious about why they feel that way.

EMOTIONAL CONTAGION

While there is no such thing as "bad" emotions because emotions are simply data, it is important to understand that feelings and behaviour in response to emotions are often contagious. Of course, I'm not talking about them being literally contagious like a disease, but people experiencing big feelings about uncertainty and change do absolutely feed off each other.

This makes dealing with the feelings of your people even more important. If you don't attend to them, expect them to grow and spread. If multiple people are negative and resistant, it can very quickly bring others down too. It's hard to stay positive when those around you fall. If you don't address the underlying emotions and fear, you can go from one or two people feeling a particular way, to the whole team becoming negative.

It's really hard to come back from this when it happens. People get sucked into the vortex and become stuck bitching and whingeing about the same thing, day in, day out. It's an energy and productivity suck. Not to mention it makes an already challenging time even more difficult.

Becoming more aware of the emotions and energy of other people can help you make decisions about who you give your time to while you lead through change. Of course, you have to spend time with your team, but outside of that you may want to become more protective. This is something I've focussed on myself over the last few years. While dealing with a lot of stress and change myself, protecting my energy has become crucial. As a result, I've pulled back from some relationships and leant into others – all based on how those people make me feel when I'm around them.

Dealing with the feelings of your people is not a fluffy extra and not something you can afford to ignore. Left unchecked, emotional contagion can make leading through change incredibly hard, and sometimes near on impossible.

WHAT'S IT LIKE TO BE AROUND ME?

Dealing with the feeling isn't just something you do for other people, it's something you must also do for yourself. You need to manage your own stress response to change or risk having your behaviour adversely impact your own health and relationships, or the health and wellbeing of others.

If you don't deal with your own feelings, they can be unleashed in damaging ways. Sometimes on our staff and colleagues but most often on the people we love the most – our families.

It's a harsh reality that those closest to us often get the worst of us. I get why – we lower our guard at home, we don't have to be "on" all the time – but the consequence can be that our partners and children bear the brunt of our emotional dysregulation. Not only can this cause tension and damage to your relationships in the home, often these escalating problems then flow back into work. It becomes a vicious cycle.

That's why three of the most powerful questions you can ask yourself are these:

1. What's it like to be around me?
2. What is the "me" experience like for my family, my partner, my children and my colleagues?
3. Am I modelling the behaviour I want to see in others?

Put down the excuses. Put down the justifications. Forget about the situation and circumstance for a moment and just answer those questions.

If you're being brutally honest with yourself, what would you say?

Sometimes the answer can be confronting.

I first heard these self-awareness questions from Australian presenter, writer and educator, Craig Harper, and oh boy – they hit like a punch in the guts. Often, we don't stop and think about the impact of our behaviour on others until it's too late.

"What's it like to be around me?" is a question I asked myself at the height of the COVID pandemic. And I did not like the answer.

I was preparing for an online workshop and had the question written out on the flip chart beside me. While I was meant to be focussed on getting ready for the training session, on that day the question stopped me in my tracks.

You see, like so many people across the world at that time, I was not at my best. I was living with the uncertainty of a global pandemic, unable to leave the house for more than an hour a day and restricted to a five-kilometre radius. My three primary school-aged boys were all at home doing remote learning – only they wouldn't do a skerrick of work unless I was sitting with them. I had transitioned my face-to-face training and speaking business to be entirely online (which meant I needed everyone in the house to be silent while I ran leadership workshops for hours on end). And my then husband was out of the house still working in his forest firefighting role.

What was it like to be around me for my family at that time? It was rubbish. I was doing all the things I teach other people NOT to do. I was stressed and yelling all the time. And because I felt so out of control I was trying to control things that really didn't matter – like how tidy the house was. When we couldn't leave it. *Insert face palm emoji*

In that moment, looking at my own writing on the flip chart, it was like a lightbulb went off. "Ohhhhh shit," I thought. "I need to practise what I preach."

I shared this story with the leadership team I worked with that very afternoon, a team of leaders from a government department who had been through the horrific Black Summer bushfires and then straight into COVID. I spoke about asking yourself these key self-awareness questions, not to beat yourself up but to ensure you are aware of the impact of your behaviour on others.

After the session, one of the leaders – Greg – reached out to me. What I'd said had hit home for him too. He had reflected on his answers to the questions and realised that he wasn't great to be around at home either. He had shut down and withdrawn from his family as a coping mechanism in response to the stress and change he had been facing at work. Not because he didn't want to be around his family, but because he wasn't ok and he hadn't been addressing how he was feeling. He was able to hold it together all day at work for his staff, but felt he had nothing left for his family. "I don't trust myself to show up well so I essentially don't show up at all," Greg told me. Admitting this was a breakthrough.

With my encouragement, Greg had a conversation with his wife and son about the challenges he was facing at work and how that was impacting him at home.

It opened up a conversation about how they could better support each other, what they needed, and how they could let each other know if it was a bad day and they would need a bit of space that night.

Facing up to and dealing with his feelings was a gamechanger for Greg and his loved ones. The vulnerability, honesty and courage it took to have the conversation resulted in greater trust, connection and understanding of each other. And because Greg acknowledged how he felt he was able to move through it with his relationships intact.

Are you aware of your own mood and feelings as you navigate change?

I encourage you to reflect on and keep track of how your emotions impact your behaviour at work and at home. You can do this in a number of ways. Here are a few suggestions to try:

1. Reflect on these key questions:

    a. What's it like to be around me?

    b. What is the "me" experience like for my staff, my colleagues, my family, my friends?

    c. Am I modelling the behaviour I want to see in others?

2. Keep a record of your mood. Check in at set times of the day or set an alarm to remind you. Note how you feel and why on a piece of paper and track it over a couple of weeks. Use the feelings wheel to help you get specific or consider downloading an app like Mood Meter.

3. Have a conversation with your partner, children and colleagues about how the change and uncertainty at work is affecting you. Share with them how you plan to keep track of your mood and ask for their help to keep you accountable. This doesn't mean you can't have bad days or have to be happy all the time, but it will make you more aware of the impact you are having on others.

While all of this may feel a bit new and even silly the first few times you do it, you may be surprised at what the reflection and mood tracking highlights for you.

Like me, you may realise that some of the behaviour you're seeing in your people started with the behaviour they saw in you.

SUMMARY

In this chapter you've learned about emotions, feelings and moods, and how they influence our response at times of uncertainty and change. You know that dealing with the feelings of your people is not optional and that by acknowledging and addressing emotions you can help them move through the change more quickly and effectively.

You appreciate that emotions and feelings are contagious and this can work for or against you. You know this means you need to be conscious of the emotions you're putting out to your team too.

You also understand that digging into and identifying the emotions and feelings that underpin a change announcement is worth it because it can help you identify the next steps in your communication and approach.

Now that you have a better insight into how your people might respond to change and how you can recognise the emotions they experience, it's time to look at how you can better respond to them by leading courageously with a balance of warmth and strength.

Chapter 4

COURAGEOUS LEADERSHIP BALANCES WARMTH AND STRENGTH

"Why does no one tell you that the people part of leadership is the hardest part?" Kylie groaned in our coaching session. "The technical part of my role is easy, it's the people bit that takes up most of my time, stress and energy."

Ahhhhh, people. Our jobs would be so easy without them, right?

Except that then there would be no one to do the work. And we wouldn't have a job anymore. Oh...

As we explored in Chapter 1, while management is about tasks, leadership is about people. And dealing with people, their emotions, challenges, behaviours and feelings takes courage.

That's why I balk at the term "soft skills', despite being known as a soft skills specialist myself. I much prefer "human" or "power" skills because there's nothing soft and easy about leading people. It's hard work.

Leading through change requires courage, not confidence. You need courageous self-leadership, courageous communication and courageous behaviour to make it through. And this courage probably looks different in action to what you'd expect.

It's not about being bold, brash, strong and commanding. It's about balancing warmth with strength, clarity with empathy, candour with compassion, and consistency with adaptability.

It's dealing with the feelings. It's being vulnerable. It's sitting with the anger and frustration of your people and then helping to lead them through to a better place. It's allowing people to express, not suppress their emotions. It's about being human yourself and connecting with the humanity of the people around you.

Confidence is easier but much less effective. You can fake confidence. I've seen many a leader attempt to bluster their way through a change only to have the curtain pulled back eventually. Like the Wizard of Oz being revealed as the madly peddling old man behind the scenes, leaders who rely on confidence without courage come unstuck. People see through the charade and realise there is very little substance behind the bold and brash front.

Leading through change requires more depth. That's not to say confidence is necessarily a bad thing, but on its own it's not enough.

In his book *Tribes: We Need You To Lead Us*, Seth Godin writes, "Leadership is scarce because few people are willing to go through the discomfort required to lead. This scarcity makes leadership valuable."

So, are you prepared to go through the discomfort required to lead? Are you up for the challenge of leading courageously through change?

The good news is, it doesn't matter whether you're confident or not. What matters is if you're prepared to be brave.

IT STARTS WITH YOU

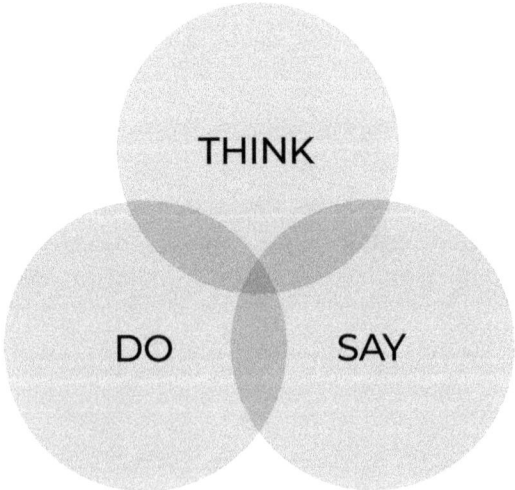

THINK

DO   SAY

Leadership is the intersection of what you think, say and do. To lead effectively you need to manage your own mindset, communication and actions – and crucially, ensure that these are all in alignment with each other. People will not listen to your words if your actions model something different. There's no point telling your people to "just calm down" if you're running around like the sky is falling down and then getting frustrated at your people for being unfocussed and stressed too. (For the record, telling a stressed person to "just calm down" is NEVER a good idea.) Your leadership success can be undermined if your mindset, words and actions are incongruent.

Kim was a leader responsible for implementing a new public land use program for her government department.

Kim thought the program was stupid – a waste of time and resources, and shouldn't be the priority senior management was telling everyone it was. She didn't hold back from sharing her view with her team either, openly undermining and ridiculing the message from the corporate office. She vented to her staff, criticised directives, and generally bagged the program to anyone who would listen.

Then, the crunch came and Kim was given two weeks to rally her staff and complete the site assessments that were required. She had to convince people to work overtime and to drop everything else they were doing in order to meet the KPIs she'd been given and get the project over the line.

Kim was in trouble. Not surprisingly, her people resisted, suggesting they deliberately not do the work as an act of defiance to what they considered to be a waste of time and an unreasonable request. An already hard task was made much more difficult by Kim's undisciplined communication and self-management over the preceding weeks. Her own words and behaviours were now biting her on the bum and she struggled to get her people to pull together. After telling them what a load of rubbish the program was, Kim was caught out trying to now convince them it had to be done. She had shot herself in the foot.

REFLECTION

Consider your own leadership through difficult times. How do you show up? How do you manage your mind, your mood, your communication, tone, body language? Honest self-awareness is key to ensuring you're showing up in a way that people are willing to follow.

ACTION

Download and complete the Communication Style Questionnaire under the Resources tab on my website to identify what your "go-to" style is under pressure and whether it may be helping or hindering your success.

ARE YOU IN OR ARE YOU OUT?

As we've already established, leading through change is tough. It requires the courage to not only be there for and deal with the feelings of your people, but also the courage to lead yourself. To face up to your own emotions and take personal responsibility for your communication and behaviour without denial, blame or justification.

That doesn't mean you'll get it right all the time or that you won't make mistakes, but you do need to ask yourself: Am I in or am I out? Am I up to the challenge and willing to do what needs to be done here even when it gets hard and uncomfortable, or not?

Once you've finished reading this book, I encourage you to answer that question honestly. Leading your people through change should be a decision you consciously make, rather than a situation you just fall into.

"Are you up for it?" I explicitly asked David, a senior leader about to navigate a wholesale restructure in his organisation. David was a handful of years off retirement and had led his people through a difficult and unpopular change five years earlier. The truth was, in David's own words it nearly broke him. He still had the mental and emotional scars from that time and he was the first to say that tough period fundamentally changed who he is.

In one of our coaching sessions, I asked David what success looked like to him at this point in his career and life, and if leading through the upcoming restructure was something he was up for. "Are you in or are you out?" I asked him plainly. "You know what it takes to lead through something like this and the impact this sort of change leadership can have on your health. You know the pressure it brings because you've been there before. Are you up for it again? Because it has to be a conscious decision if you want to do it well."

This made David pause and reflect. Up until that moment David hadn't consciously considered whether leading through this upcoming change was something he even wanted to do. He hadn't stopped and asked himself that question. He hadn't realised he had a choice and that making that choice was critical to him having any chance of leading successfully. He decided he was in.

This simple act of committing to leading his people through the change changed David's mindset towards it. Rather than it being something that he had to do or that was happening to him, it was something he was choosing to do. I want you to make a conscious choice too.

If you're in, you need to be prepared to weather the storm. You have to understand there will be ups and downs, for you and your people, and that it won't all be smooth sailing. You have to be prepared to show up, own the message, be vulnerable, get curious, show people you care, and cop criticism. It's a lot.

But if you're up for the challenge, leading through change can be the making, not breaking of you. Nothing builds trust and respect like guiding your people through tough times when a lesser leader would abandon ship.

If you're out, if what you've read up to this point has made you realise that leading through change is not for you, you are better to put your hand up now and own it. It takes courage to say no and admit you're not up for the job. That's not weakness, that's strength. Leaders who should say no to the challenge of leading through change but don't can do serious damage to their own physical and mental health and also that of their people.

If you are in, understand it won't just be business as usual when you lead through change. You'll need to find an inner strength and courage to give more than you've ever given before emotionally. It's important to make a conscious commitment to lead through change so you are able to stay the course and remain focussed when challenged. This will give you the grounding to come back to when things get hard. It will be tough but it will almost always be worth it.

LOOK AFTER YOURSELF

In order to be able to show up well, manage your own stress and lead your people through change, I want you to consider the supports you need put in place for yourself. You need to be ok in the middle of the shitstorm. What will help you do that? Don't be too proud to think you have to struggle through on your own without help.

Think about the support you can put in place at work, at home and in your social life as you lead through change. There's no right or wrong answer to this. Every person is different. I've listed some examples below to get you started, but by no means is it exhaustive. You need to consider what's right for you. And the key is to put them in place proactively, now, before you need them. Don't wait to not be ok to reach out for help. If you know change or a challenging time is approaching, set those supports up now.

Self-care is not a luxury when it comes to leading through change. It's essential.

If you go down, in many cases, so will your team. Pushing through is not a sustainable option. Sure, resilience and a stoic approach can be powerful, but looking after yourself is crucial too. To lead at your best, you need to be at your best.

WORK

▸ **Hold regular leadership meetings to talk about LEADERSHIP.** Meet regularly with other leaders affected by the change to specifically focus on LEADERSHIP. This meeting is not about the nuts and bolts of the change itself or where the process is up to, but rather focussed on the people bit.

▸ **Hire a mentor or coach.**

- ▸ **Create an out-of-hours communication strategy.**
  Have a conversation with your team about how you want to be communicated with out of hours. For example, tell your people if there is an emergency or something that needs a response, they need to phone or text message you, not email. This will help you to be able to keep out of your email at home when you need to disconnect.

- ▸ **Engage with your Employee Assistance Program (EAP) if your organisation has one.**
  You don't have to be unwell to get support.

- ▸ **Put boundaries in place.**
  Ensure work doesn't creep into all aspects of your life by putting some boundaries in place, such as no work on Sundays. Being able to disconnect and recharge is critical.

- ▸ **Schedule your priorities, don't prioritise your schedule (thanks Stephen Covey).**
  When leading through change it's easy to become reactionary and frantic. Take time each day, or each Friday, to put the most important things into your calendar for the next day or week. That includes putting lunch in as an appointment and scheduling time for leadership. A common frustration of leaders during times of change is that they don't have time to do the people bit because tasks and management take over. Schedule 30 to 60 minutes a day for people stuff.

- ▸ **Use your out of office when you're in meetings all day or off-site, even if you're still working.**
  Include a brief explanation of what you're doing and then set expectations for when you can likely respond. For example:
  I am in meetings all day so my response to email may be delayed. If the matter is urgent, please text my mobile on xxxxxxxx.

PERSONAL

▸ **Get enough sleep.**
The research on the impact of sleep on our cognitive and physical functioning is unequivocal. Without enough sleep you may as well be leading drunk.

▸ **Eat well.**
Boring, I know. But binging on junk food because you're too stressed and time poor will likely see you crash and burn. You need to fuel your body well to ensure your brain functions at its best and you have the energy to see the change through.

▸ **Exercise.**
For your mental health more than your physical health. Get outside if you can and move in whatever way works for you – be it team sport, walking, running, lifting weights, whatever! Exercise is a great form of stress relief – it not only burns off cortisol (the stress hormone) but also gets the endorphins (happy hormones) flowing. Bonus points if you can do it outside in nature.

▸ **Find healthy ways to process your emotions and turn off.**
This looks different for everyone but is not about numbing out with alcohol, drugs, social media or smoking. Think more about putting your phone away at a certain time each night, playing with your pets, watching your favourite TV show, and listening to your favourite music.

▸ **Ask for support from your nearest and dearest.**
Speak to your family and friends about the pressure the change is going to put you under and ask for their help and support to help you manage your wellbeing. This is also a good opportunity to set expectations with your loved ones for the change period. If your availability is going to be limited or you're likely to be distracted and quieter, let them know this.

LEAD WITH WARMTH FIRST, STRENGTH SECOND

If you want the best chance of your people following you as you steer them through the storm of challenge and change, lead with warmth first, strength second. Both are core to your leadership success, but the order in which you apply them in is important.

In the article 'Connect, Then Lead', published by Amy Cuddy, Matthew Kohut and John Neffinger in the July–August 2013 issue of *Harvard Business Review*, the trio outline why the key to communicating with influence for leaders is to begin with warmth (think empathy, trust, care and compassion) and then follow with strength. They found that warmth contributes more significantly to others' evaluation of us than competence and strength. Why? Because warmth conveys our underlying intention. It shows the person receiving your communication that you care about them as a human and have their interests at heart – even if the message you're delivering is difficult to hear.

Warmth builds respect and if someone respects you, they are more likely to cooperate, follow and align themselves with you.

Unfortunately, warmth tends to get pushed to the side in times of pressure, such as when you're communicating news of significant change – like a restructure. The focus instead is often on projecting strength, with some leaders even worrying that kindness and concern will be seen as weak and soft. As I wrote in *Soft is the New Hard*, the logic seems to be, "Just tell them the facts and keep it cold, direct and specific. That way they know we're serious and this is the way it's going to be."

The problem is, if you lead with strength and no warmth, you lose one of the most important things you have at your disposal: the discretionary effort of your people. According to Cuddy, Kohut and Neffinger, when strength and competence come before, or without, warmth in your communication, trust is undermined. While people may comply with the change publicly, privately they are more likely to disengage, feel resentful and lack respect for you. You may get what you want in the short term but the damage you do to your relationships with people in your team can be terminal.

When you rely on aggression and intimidation to get your own way, your people may do what you ask out of fear and obligation to comply but they'll do no more than that. They won't go over and above for you and some may even start deliberately undermining you as a way of passive-aggressively making their anger and frustration known.

During the second year of the COVID pandemic, many leaders thought the worst was over and wanted people to return to the office. While some organisations navigated this well by listening to their staff and dealing with their various feelings, others jumped straight to blanket "return to work" directives, with no explanation as to why this was required, despite people having proven they could work effectively from home for the 12 months prior. It was all strength, no warmth.

Not surprisingly, those who took the steamroller approach quickly found themselves in trouble. I fielded many a call from leaders struggling with loud resistance from their people and trying to work out a compromise and win back trust AFTER their initial "just tell them" approach blew up in their face.

Leading with warmth means you see the human first and the task second.

- It's showing your people that you genuinely care about them and their wellbeing, and making sure your words, tone, body language and actions all convey that.
- It's taking the time to check in and see how they're travelling.
- It's empathising, acknowledging that change is challenging, asking questions and showing interest in their response.

As Maya Angelou famously said, "People won't remember what you say and do, but they will remember how you made them feel." How you lead through change will often come to define what people think of your leadership. And when you finally make it out the other side, people will always remember how you made them feel in the middle of the storm.

Leading with warmth makes people feel valued and cared for. Then, when you add strength in second by driving the change and holding people accountable, they are more likely to stick with you – even if they don't like the change itself.

Being a strong leader during uncertain and challenging times is important. Warmth without being decisive, competent and directional can see you manipulated, walked all over, and out of control as a leader. You may be seen as weak, soft and someone to be pitied. You don't want that either. But while strength and competence are important, Cuddy, Kohut and Neffinger argue you should always lead with warmth first.

YOU'RE NOT A MAGICIAN, YOU CAN'T DO IT FOR THEM

Leading through change with courage and a balance of warmth and strength gets results, but it's important to remember that you're not a magician and you can't do the impossible. And therein lies a key challenge – you must be conscious of the fact that you can't control other people, you can only control you – your own response, mindset, communication, feelings, actions and behaviour (and you have a responsibility to do that). You can't control how your people react to the change but you can absolutely influence it. And that's your job. As a leader you can INFLUENCE how your people navigate change.

During times of uncertainty, people look to their leaders for guidance, and the amount of influence you have over their reactions will depend on the trust and relationships you've already built, plus the behaviour and communication you model. You can provide them with the reassurance that you care, are there for them, and will lead them through the change if they're willing to follow. But you can't make them follow and you can't make them be ok. You can guide and coach your people but you can't rescue them if they don't want to be saved. They have to be willing to save themselves.

No matter what the change, there is an element of personal responsibility that underpins each individual's response. Yes, as the leader you will do your best to lead courageously – to be frank, fair and transparent – but people are responsible for their own actions, reactions and behaviour.

I want you to read the above paragraphs again. This needs to sink in and be crystal clear to you.

You must understand what is and isn't your responsibility as a leader so you can focus on what you can influence and control, rather than be distracted by or waste your time and energy on things you can't change.

I have seen too many leaders crash and burn as they desperately try to save those around them during a crisis, change, or period of high pressure and uncertainty. They tie themselves in knots playing the rescuer and the people pleaser while those in their team play the hapless victims. The harsh reality is you can't help someone who won't help themselves – you'll just kill yourself trying. And then you're no help to anyone.

We'll be looking more deeply into this in Chapter 7, but to get you started here's an action you can take right now.

ACTION

Consider a change or challenge you're leading through at the moment and then make a three-column list like the one on the next page. Fill out each column with the specifics in relation to this challenge:

► What you can control? (This is limited to what you can do.)

► What you can influence? (This is about your relationships and communication.)

► What do you need to let go of? (What are you wasting time worrying about that you have no control or influence over and need to let go of?)

What can I control?	What can I influence?	What do I need to let go of?

VULNERABILITY IS STRENGTH, NOT WEAKNESS

Leading courageously through change also requires vulnerability and vulnerability takes guts.

What does vulnerability look like when you're leading through change?

▸ It's being prepared to show up and risk emotional exposure when you don't have all the answers and you're not sure about the change yourself.

▸ It's being prepared to stand up and lead when you're scared and want to hide.

▸ It's facing the hurt, confusion and anger of your people with care and compassion.

▸ It's admitting you're scared and acknowledging your own feelings, while also assuring your team that you're right in there with them. You don't know if it'll all be ok, but you do know that you will be there to guide them through.

▸ It's owning your mistakes and admitting when you get it wrong. It's being prepared to change your mind when you get new information.

Vulnerability – something that was once considered a weakness (in fact, you may have been raised and taught that as a leader you SHOULDN'T show vulnerability) is now almost universally acknowledged to be a sign of great strength. It shows your people you're human. It creates connection and fosters trust and respect. It assures your people that you're there for them, even though things are tough.

During the COVID pandemic, leaders worldwide at all levels were suddenly forced into a position of great vulnerability. No one had been through anything like this before and no one knew for certain how to best respond. Everyone was making it up as they went along, based on the information they had at the time.

The best leaders stood up in the face of this worldwide uncertainty, were prepared to make the big and hard calls when needed, showed empathy, admitted they were giving it their best guess based on the advice they received, and were also prepared to make changes and adjustments based on new information as it came to hand. Think Angela Merkel in Germany and Jacinda Ardern in New Zealand.

The worst hedged their bets, procrastinated on decisions, pretended there was no issue or problem (pandemic? What pandemic), or bulldozed their decisions through without an ounce of empathy to be seen. This bullish, petulant combination of steamroller and shirker leadership was best encompassed by Donald Trump.

1. Consider a time you've seen a leader stand up and be vulnerable at a time of great pressure and stress. How did it make you feel? What did it make you think of their leadership? Were they someone you wanted to follow?

2. On the flipside, consider when you've seen a leader refuse to acknowledge their own humanity in a crisis. When they've been like stone – hard and cold – or refused emotional exposure. How did that make you feel? What did you think of their leadership as a result? Did their approach bring you comfort or greater fear?

3. Now, consider which leader you want to be as you lead your people through change. Let's face it, if you didn't choose vulnerability, this is not the book for you.

SUMMARY

Having read this far, you now understand what it takes to lead both yourself and others through change. You've seen the Five Cs® model on which the rest of this book is based and you haven't run scared. You know it's not going to be easy and that following every strategy outlined in this book does not guarantee you success. But you also know that leading courageously through change is the best chance you've got of weathering the storm and you're prepared to give it a crack.

You're prepared to learn and you're prepared to do the hard work required to step up as a courageous leader. Now it's time to buckle up as I teach you the HOW of communicating and leading through challenge and change.

That's what the rest of this book is devoted to – outlining each element of my Five Cs® model in detail with practical strategies, scripts and actions to help you put your learning into practice and get results.

PART 2

HOW

Chapter 5

CREATE CLARITY

The Five Cs

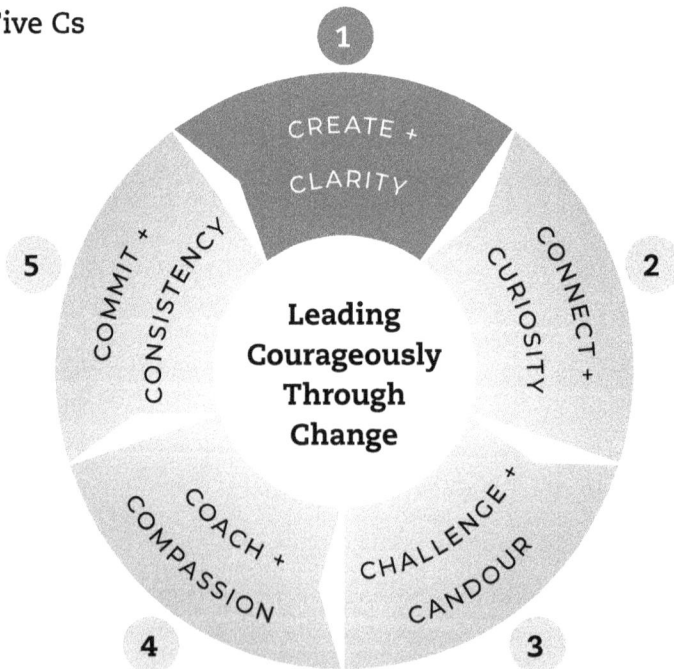

Create: "To bring into being; cause to exist; produce." *– Macquarie Dictionary*

Clarity: "The quality of being clear and easy to understand, see or hear." *– Cambridge Dictionary*

Uncertainty is unnerving. The first step to leading courageously through change is to create clarity for yourself so you can then provide clarity for your people.

Even if people don't like the change, if they understand what it is, why it's needed, and have the message delivered in a frank, transparent, proactive and empathetic way, they are more likely to get on board. It's about telling the truth with kindness. As Brené Brown says, clear is kind.

On the flipside, unclear is unkind and in cases where there is no communication at all, where conversations about the change are avoided, information is withheld and people are left in the dark – it is downright cruel.

Even if delaying the release of information is well intentioned, if you don't communicate clearly and provide context to explain why the change is needed, people can:

- ▸ Become disillusioned.
- ▸ Get hit harder later on (because the change was unexpected and they were unprepared).
- ▸ Stress more about what's coming because of the uncertainty created.
- ▸ Lose trust in you as their leader.
- ▸ Be overcome by feelings of anxiousness, fear and anger.
- ▸ Be distracted by the change which leads to low productivity and gossip.
- ▸ Anticipate something far worse than is actually proposed.

A large industrial site was on the eve of a major restructure. Everyone knew something big was brewing and talk of a restructure was everywhere. But while people knew large-scale change was coming, staff and even most senior leaders were in the dark about what it was, what it would look like and who would be impacted.

In the vacuum of information, people created their own stories and the lack of clarity led to speculation, gossip, rumour and a sense of gross distrust of management. It also put mid-range leaders in a very difficult position. While they were as clueless as their staff about what was coming, most staff assumed they knew more (despite their protests) and were hiding it from them. When the restructure was finally announced some months later, it still lacked the detail of how it would be implemented, which further inflamed tensions on site.

A lack of communication early meant the change was demonised before it begun, and when the messaging did finally flow it was dismissed as reactive damage control.

Before you can create clarity about the change to your team, you need to get clear yourself. That means doing the thinking about:

- How you want to lead through the change and what you want to be known for as a leader during this challenging time.
- Your vision for how you want to navigate the change as an individual and as a team.
- The questions you need to ask up the chain to ensure you have as much information and context as possible so you are clear and can answer the questions of your team.

Once you have clarity for yourself, it is crucial you create as much clarity as possible for your people. The more they understand the change and the more prepared they are for it, the better.

Now, at this point you may be yelling at the pages in this book, "But Leah, I don't have all the information to be able to provide my team with clarity!" The good news is, even when things are uncertain and you don't have all the answers yourself, you can still provide clarity for your team in other ways.

Being honest and transparent in your communication during change will build trust in you as a leader, even if your team is losing trust in the organisation because they don't know what's going to happen. By clarifying what you can, you will help give your people a feeling of stability, which they are likely to be desperately seeking.

GET CLEAR YOURSELF

As Stephen Covey said in his classic book *The 7 Habits of Highly Effective People*: "Begin with the end in mind."

I'm not talking about where you want to end up with the change itself, but how you want to lead through the change yourself, and where you hope to get your people to.

If you don't start with a clear vision for how you want to show up and lead, it's easy to quickly end up off course and be led by other people's reactions instead.

When this happens you may not recognise the person you've become and often that's not a good thing. It may not be your intention but other people's perception of you may also be at total odds with the person you want to be.

Get clear on the sort of leader, colleague, employee, family member and friend you want to be through the change so you can then make a choice to show up in a way that contributes towards that.

This strategy was the foundational tool that guided me through significant challenges and change in my own life. I got clear on who I wanted to be, how I wanted to show up, and what I wanted to be known for during the challenging time. I then used this as my guiding light, my north star, for my communication and behaviour.

REFLECTION

Consider how you want to lead through the change or challenge you are facing and ask yourself:

- ▸ What do I want to be known for?
- ▸ What do I want my team to say about me and my leadership when I'm not in the room?
- ▸ What do I want the experience of being around me to be like for my staff, colleagues, family, friends?
- ▸ How do I want to make people feel?
- ▸ What behaviour do I need to model to be known for this?
- ▸ What don't I want to do/be known for (think about the poor examples of leading through change that you've experienced before)?
- ▸ What outcome do I want and why is it important?
- ▸ How do I want my people to navigate and emerge from this change?
- ▸ What is my vision for success?
- ▸ What does successfully leading myself through this change look like?

PROVIDE CLARITY FOR YOUR TEAM

Once you've done this thinking, consider what answers you could share with your team. This is particularly important if there is a lot of uncertainty and unknown about the change. Any information you can give them, even if it's not about the change itself but rather how you plan to lead them through it, can provide much-needed reassurance at times of stress.

If you're wondering what sort of information you can provide to your team, even if you don't have all the information (or any information) about the detail of the change yet, here are some suggestions:

- ▸ How you want to lead your team through change.
- ▸ What outcome you want for your team.
- ▸ Your vision for how your team navigates the change. Better yet, develop it with them and unite behind it.
- ▸ What you don't want to do (use storytelling to highlight).
- ▸ The timeline (key points).
- ▸ Next steps.
- ▸ What is and isn't ok behaviour-wise.
- ▸ What they can influence and the choices available (what's up for negotiation and what's not – provide a menu if possible).

- Your expectations of them (for example, if they have questions or concerns, you want them to raise them with you).

- How the leadership team wants to navigate the change (key messages).

Don't underestimate the power of creating a shared vision for how your team navigates the change. Having a strong vision or purpose to unite behind can be the making or breaking of a team at times of stress.

Prior to COVID, I had been engaged by the CEO of a community-owned aged care facility to deliver communication and leadership training in a bid to improve culture and working relationships among staff. Aged care is notoriously poorly paid and staff are often under stress, which can play out with niggles, bitchiness and poor behaviour, as it did at this facility.

And then COVID hit.

Aged care has always been important, but suddenly these staff were on the frontline trying to protect some of the most vulnerable people in our community from the virus. Residents were locked in their rooms and staff wearing full PPE became their only physical contact with the outside world. These staff were under incredible pressure and also bore the terrifying stress that they might unintentionally bring the virus into the facility.

Yet something interesting happened amongst this team. Despite the incredible pressure, stress, fatigue and fear they all faced, the petty bitchiness and people problems that existed before the pandemic melted away. They had something much bigger and more important to focus on. The leaders created and reiterated their core purpose to staff on every shift, and the staff rallied. They united behind that purpose – protecting the most vulnerable – and rather than heighten the fractures that were already there, the pandemic brought perspective and a sense of unity that had not existed before.

The challenge post pandemic of course, was for them to retain as much of that unity and sense of purpose as possible. The executive did this by revisiting the organisation's purpose with staff in the months after lockdown. They had seen first-hand how powerful clarity was for the team's success.

REFLECTION

What is the shared purpose of your team that you want them to unite behind as they navigate change? Why do you exist and why is steering through the storm so important?

Being clear on this will help you to engage the hearts and minds of your people by communicating in a way that speaks to their emotions, motivations and drivers.

BAD NEWS IS BETTER THAN NO NEWS

We've all heard the saying "no news is good news" but often, particularly when you know change is brewing, that is NOT the case. In fact, not only is no news not good news, frequently, it is even WORSE than bad news, because it creates uncertainty.

As highlighted in Chapter 2, it can be tempting to avoid the elephant in the room when communicating change, perhaps because you know it will be unpopular, you don't have all the answers, you're not the one instigating the change, or you know there is no "win" in it for your people. You don't want your team to shoot the messenger so it can feel safer to stay silent. But avoidance and silence only makes problems grow.

If you don't own bad news and give it context, people fill the space with their own stories and conclusions based on fear, rumour and innuendo, and their personal reaction to uncertainty. Often those stories are far worse than what is actually planned.

Our fear of the unknown is often worse than the fear of the change itself when it is finally revealed. This negative bias is a result of evolution.

Our brain is wired to identify threats and focus on danger in a bid to keep us safe, so it's no surprise that our people go there.

According to Hilary Scarlett, author of *Neuroscience for Organisational Change*, the brain finds uncertainty so uncomfortable that we are better at dealing with bad news than not knowing what the future holds.

Rick was made redundant in a restructure. "Finding out I was being made redundant and being given the information about the package I would receive as a result was actually a relief," he said. "The period in between, when we knew a restructure was coming and that jobs would be lost, but we didn't know how many and we didn't know what the payout would be – that period of not knowing was agony. I didn't sleep for weeks."

As David Rock and Christy Pruitt-Haynes wrote in *Harvard Business Review*: "Research shows that getting an answer you don't like is better than not receiving one at all. Any way you can provide useful information, even if it seems small, can increase people's sense of clarity, if not certainty."

So, my suggestion is this: share as much truth as you can – even if it's not what people want to hear – because this builds trust.

But what if sharing is not allowed? What if you've been sworn to secrecy and your people ask questions you're not allowed to answer? Again – the answer is simple, speak the truth. Don't say

"I don't know," if you do. This is a sure-fire way to erode trust if your people know or suspect that this is a lie and you're simply not telling them. Instead:

▸ Be transparent: *"I can't share that information with you."*

▸ Empathise, but stay firm to your message: *"I appreciate you want more information and this uncertainty is unnerving but at this stage I am unable to share any more detail."*

▸ Include the *"why"* if you can. It may be: *"Because the final structure has not yet been finalised"*, *"Because it's commercial in-confidence"*, *"Because we're still working through what the change will look like"*.

▸ Outline your commitment to keeping them as informed as you can: *"My promise to you is that I will be as open and honest as I can be with you and communicate any updates as soon as I have them."*

A FOUR-PART FRAMEWORK FOR COMMUNICATING IN UNCERTAINTY

The words "honesty" and "transparency" are often used inter-changeably. But there's a difference between the two and in times of uncertainty, transparency is what people are after.

Honesty is telling the truth as you perceive it and refusing to lie or be deceptive – crucially – when you're asked. Transparency means easy to see through. If you are being transparent, you are sharing the truth that you believe needs to be known because it's the right thing to do. You're not waiting to be asked, you are being open in your communication and proactively sharing.

In that awkward period when you know change is coming but you don't know exactly what it looks like yet, transparency is a powerful trust and respect-building tool.

So how do you communicate with transparency to your team when things are uncertain? Here is a simple four-step framework to help you.

Tell them:

1. What we know.

2. What we're doing about it.

3. What we don't know.

4. When we expect to know and how we will keep you informed.

I have used this framework with many leadership teams over the years, including leaders at a large disability service provider facing looming government changes that had the potential to leave its staff without jobs. Here's what the framework looked like in practice in the key messages delivered at an all-staff briefing:

1. **What we know:**
   - ▸ The federal government is changing the way it funds aged care.

   - ▸ These changes will be implemented from 1 July.

   - ▸ The government is in the discovery phase, running workshops to get input.

   - ▸ We expect a detailed announcement of changes by the end of the year.

   - ▸ There will be a single assessment service.

   - ▸ Assessors will set the amount of service a customer gets.

2. **What we're doing about it:**

- ▸ We are keeping up to date with any announcements and sending leaders to all government briefings and update meetings.

- ▸ We are providing input to government at every opportunity we can.

- ▸ We are doing the strategic work now to ensure we are best positioned to deal with the changes when they come.

3. **What we don't know:**

- ▸ What the changes look like or how they will impact us.

- ▸ What happens with our existing clients (if they are grandfathered) or a timeline for them to transition to the new system.

- ▸ What jobs will look like.

- ▸ What funding we'll have.

- ▸ If we'll be the provider.

- ▸ If some of our services are viable going forward.

4. **When we expect to know and how we will keep you informed:**

- ▸ We expect to have an update from government with further information in the coming months.

- ▸ Our commitment to you is to share that information with you as soon as we have it.

- ▸ In the meantime, we are investing in training to help you self-manage through change to ensure you're able to get through this uncertain time in the best shape possible.

WHAT IF YOU CAN'T SHARE THE REASONS BEHIND A CHANGE?

Sarah, the CEO of a tech company, prided herself on being a very open leader. Her team never had to wonder about her agenda or if she had an ulterior motive because she was always transparent in her communication.

Until she couldn't be.

Sarah had to sack a senior leader for gross misconduct. It wasn't pretty. The leader had to pack up their desk immediately and be escorted from the building by a security guard. "It was like a scene from a movie," she told me. "I was devastated it came to that."

What made the situation even worse was Sarah couldn't share the reasons for the leader's departure with her team, or explain why he'd had to be escorted from the building. "That was really, really hard," she said. "I've always prided myself on being a very open person and now I was in a position where I couldn't share information with my people or tell them why this key leader, who many of them liked as a person as well as a leader, was sacked in such dramatic fashion."

So what did Sarah do? She couldn't share the details with her team or would risk being sacked herself. But did that mean she had to say nothing at all? No it did not.

"Thankfully I had consciously invested in building a strong relationship of trust with my people for many years," Sarah explained. "So what I did was pull the team together and say, 'You're just going to have to have faith in me that I've got the business from where it was to where it is today and we've made a lot of good decisions along the way. We've always put culture and behaviour ahead of results, sales performance, or profit and loss. I'm asking you to trust me that we had to make this decision and it was the right one to make. I will never shy away from a tough decision if not making it would impact on our culture negatively.'"

Although she couldn't share the reasons for the decision and her people were still going to speculate and be dissatisfied with the answer, Sarah had the courage to provide what clarity and context she could to her team. And because she had a foundation of trust, most were willing to go with her.

KNOW YOUR AUDIENCE: IT'S ABOUT THEM, NOT YOU

A mistake that many leaders make when communicating change is to focus on saying what they want to say, and parroting the official company line, rather than considering the audience and what they want to hear.

Don't get me wrong – I'm not suggesting you go rogue and stray from the company message (I'm not looking to get you fired!). What I am suggesting is that you consider your audience and provide context for your message that is relevant to your people. One size does not necessarily fit all when communicating change and it is important that the messaging is tailored to the people it is being delivered to.

A good place to start is considering:

1. What outcome do I want?
2. How can I tailor my communication to give me the best

chance of achieving that outcome considering the audience I'm delivering it to?

Considering the outcome you're after will help you pause and think about the best approach for leading your people through change. It's not about your preference and style, this is about considering your audience and communicating in a way that they are most likely to respond well to.

To help answer the second question above and get into your people's heads, consider the following "who, what, when, where, why, how" questions about your audience:

Who

- ▸ Who is my audience? (Direct reports only or are you speaking to their families and the community too?)

- ▸ Who should be part of the conversation? (One-on-one or in a group?)

What

- ▸ What do they care about?

- ▸ What are their drivers and motivators?

- ▸ What sort of language do they use?

- ▸ What's going on for them? What is the context into which this message will be delivered?

- ▸ What emotions are they likely to experience? (Use this to inject empathy by acknowledging the emotion.)

- ▸ What do they respond well to? How do they like to receive messages?

- ▸ What don't they respond well to?

- ▸ What's in it for them?

When

▸ When is it best to have this conversation? When will you deliver the message? (Don't save it up. Make it timely.)

Where

▸ Where should you have this conversation? Should it be in a neutral location? A private office? At a pre-start?

Why

▸ Why do you need to have this conversation?

▸ Why now?

▸ Why should they care?

How

▸ How are your people impacted?

▸ How should you frame the conversation?

▸ How should you deliver the message? (Should it be an email, a face-to-face conversation, a team meeting, a video call, over the phone?)

▸ How are they likely to react?

▸ How will you respond if they ask curly questions or respond poorly?

A word of warning here: don't overthink it. While this list includes important things to consider about your audience, your approach and your message before communicating change to your team, it's also important to not get bogged down in overthinking or to become immobilised at the thought of getting it wrong.

Remember, there is no one definitive right way to communicate a change and there is no way of guaranteeing that your message will be well received. You can't control how your people react, you can only influence it. So do ask yourself the questions, consider your answers and spend time doing the thinking first, but then be courageous and have the conversation – whether it goes well or not.

Considering his audience was something business owner Andy McCarthy had to get his head around quickly in 2019 after announcing to his team of 75 staff at Gippsland Solar that they were being acquired by RACV Solar.

Andy, who went on to be the CEO of RACV Solar, started Gippsland Solar from the spare bedroom of his house with his wife Kelly in 2010. They hired their first employees in 2013 and grew exponentially in the next five years, meaning Andy was no stranger to leading his team through rapid change.

Despite this, announcing the acquisition was big and unsettling news and Andy had to consider how best to communicate it in order to get his staff onboard. His team was going from working for a capital-constrained husband and wife business where it's easy to buy into the vision and the 'why' to having new ownership thrust upon them and working for a large corporate entity.

"It took me a little while to really come to terms with how to sell the message because when you're standing there in front of your team telling them, 'This is the best thing that's ever happened to us,' they go, 'Well, you just had a payday so of course you'd say that, whereas our lives have been turned around and we haven't been given a payday.'

"I realised I had to look at it through their lens. I had to think about each of those people in each of their roles and ask myself, 'Why is this a positive change for them? What are they going to get?'

"They were never going to get the benefit from the sale that my wife and I would as business owners, so I had to think about what opportunities the acquisition would create for them and take our own personal bias out of it. I had to remember my audience and communicate what was in it for them."

In the four years after Gippsland Solar was acquired by RACV Solar, Andy led the acquisition of another three solar businesses across Victoria and expanded his team of employees from 75 to 170.

Every time he expanded the business, Andy made a conscious decision to put himself in the shoes of staff – both those already at RACV Solar and those at the business being acquired – and he considered the change from their perspective. This allowed him to develop messaging that provided clarity, connection and a sense of calm to people.

The fact that RACV Solar maintained employee engagement scores in the high 60s in those four years was a great measure of that success.

REFLECTION

Put yourself in your people's position and consider what they want to know, the questions they'll have, and how you can best answer them.

Communication is only effective if the message is heard, so forget for a moment what you want to tell your team about the change and instead think about what it is that they want to hear and what impact the change will have on them.

PRE-EMPT CURLY QUESTIONS WITH Q&A SPARRING

You should never go into a conversation with your people about change thinking, "Jeez, I hope they don't ask this..." because you can almost guarantee that question will come up. Do the thinking first and be prepared. This is where an activity I call Q&A sparring can be incredibly useful. Here's how it works:

▶ Get together with a colleague, or even a trusted family member, present the change or challenge to them and ask them to throw the curliest questions they have back at you.

▶ Don't try to answer them at this point, just collect the questions in a big, long list.

▶ Then, go away and consider how you could answer them, or better yet, how you could proactively seed them into your messaging. If you pre-empt and answer those tough questions in a meeting with your people without even being asked, you will build further trust because you've shown them that you really understand their concerns.

You may not be able to answer every question you uncover doing this activity, and that's ok.

What you can do for those really curly ones is develop a simple holding response such as: *"I appreciate you have many questions about the detail of the change but unfortunately at this point I don't have those answers for you."*

This will help you to feel calmer, less nervous and more in control going into a challenging conversation about the change.

QUESTIONS TO CONSIDER (AND ANSWER) IN YOUR MESSAGING

Once you've answered the "who, what, when, where, why, how" questions for your audience, and done the Q&A sparring activity, it is useful to apply the same "who, what, when, where, why, how " framework to the actual change message itself.

When communicating the change, the key things your people will want to know include:

Who

▸ Who is impacted by the change?

What

▸ What is the change?

▸ What does it mean for them?

▸ What's in it for them?

▸ What (if anything) can they influence?

▸ What happens if they don't change? (Tread carefully here. You don't want it to be a threat.)

▸ What happens if they do change? What are the benefits?

▸ What options do they have? (People don't like being told what to do.)

▸ What's your key message?

When

▸ When is it happening?

▸ When will they know more?

Where

▸ Where is it happening? Where are the changes being made? In what part of the business?

Why

- ▸ Why is it happening? Why is the change needed? (Provide the context and if possible, make it compelling to your audience and speak to their personal motivations and drivers.)
- ▸ Why now?
- ▸ Why is it important?
- ▸ Why should they care?
- ▸ Why should they get on board and navigate the change in the way you suggest?

How

- ▸ How will it impact them?
- ▸ How will the change be rolled out?
- ▸ How can they get involved, provide feedback, have a say, or influence implementation?
- ▸ How will you keep them updated throughout the change process?

EMPHASISE THE WHY

If people understand the reason for the change and the context in which it fits, even if they don't like the change itself, they will be more likely to live with it. A strong "why" will help them come to acceptance.

Focussing on the "why" is how Cynthia approached her messaging when she introduced a new key performance indicator for billable hours with her National Disability Insurance Scheme team.

KPIs and billable hours are never popular and there was a high chance that the change would cause uproar in Cynthia's team of contract staff. Her people liked taking their time with NDIS clients. Most got into the industry to support people with disabilities and make a difference in their lives, not to charge by the minute or hour like lawyers. But the reality was, Cynthia's team was haemorrhaging money and the service was unsustainable if left as it was. If Cynthia buried her head in the sand and did not take action, all of their jobs were at risk. So, Cynthia explained this to her team. She was open and transparent about the situation and explained why having a KPI for each staff member to reach five billable hours per day would help ensure the future of the program and balance service to clients with efficiency.

Cynthia took the time to make sure her people understood the reason why the change was required and developed messaging that was relevant to them. Of course her team wanted to continue supporting clients (something they couldn't do if the program was shut down for being unsustainable), and of course her people also wanted to keep their jobs (something they also couldn't do if the program was shut down). Although no one was thrilled with the new KPIs, everyone understood why they were required and was prepared to adhere to the change.

As a result, Cynthia was able to improve her team's performance, attract further government funding for the team, and help all her contract staff become ongoing employees at the organisation – things that would not have happened if the change hadn't been adopted.

While the "why" is often the superpower move that gets people over the line to accept change, albeit begrudgingly, it's not always enough. As Zoë Routh wrote in her book *People Stuff*: "People will campaign against ethical change if their own self interests are at stake. We saw this in all big social reforms like slavery and segregation. Appealing to people's higher nature did not always win over opponents if it meant privilege and benefits were at stake."

Now, if you're the meat in the sandwich, the middle manager delivering the message, there is a possibility (if your leaders have communicated poorly) that you don't have a good understanding of the "why" behind the change yourself. If that's the case, stop. Don't deliver the message to your team without the "why". Go back to your leader and ask up the chain for the "why" to be explained. How you go about doing this will influence your success here. I'm not suggesting you go back to your leader and aggressively ask, "Why?!? Tell me why this is happening?" What I am suggesting is you go back to your leader, your board or whoever is driving the change and frame the question a little something like this:

"To help me to communicate this change to the team and give us the best chance of them receiving it well, can you please share more about the reason behind this decision? If my people understand the context in which it sits, they are more likely to accept it and less likely to resist."

See what I did there? I considered my audience (your manager) and spoke to their motivations and drivers. While the decision-makers may not care whether your people like the change or not, you can bet they care whether your people resist it or not, because this has potential to impact the success of the change and the organisation's bottom line.

GIVE IT TO THEM STRAIGHT

People can smell bullshit a mile away. Give it to them straight – don't spin it. Even if you do the considered thinking first, you can lose people immediately if you try to get clever with your messaging or disguise harsh realities of change with fluffy descriptions of "wins" that aren't there.

Be as proactive, transparent, authentic, clear and "plain speak" as possible in your communication. Share the complete truth, even if it's not what people want to hear. While they might not like it, your honesty will build trust.

When Steve, a leader in the power industry, explained the reasons for a department restructure to his team, he gave it to them straight.

"The reality is, we want to stay open as long as possible," Steve explained to his crew. "Yes, we have a proposed closure date that is still 10 to 15 years away, but that is not a given. If we don't make changes to operate more effectively before then, the reality is we could go sooner. The days when we could rail against any change are over. We're on a good wicket here and if we want to continue to be for as long as we can, then we need to be willing to adapt and adjust."

Steve didn't sugar-coat it. He presented the reality to his team in a frank way, with the context in which the change was being made at the forefront of his message.

BE PROACTIVE

Get out ahead of the change with your messaging if you can. Don't wait for the change to arrive or questions to be asked to communicate your message. Delaying your announcement often makes the shock of change worse (that said, there can be times when delaying is appropriate if it means you are able to answer more questions and have more detailed information when you do make the change announcement).

Yes, being proactive can be scary, but it also allows you to have more control of the messaging, rather than be caught on the back foot responding to media leaks or workplace rumours.

KEEP IT SIMPLE

Keep your explanations and word choices as simple and clear as possible. Don't use jargon, corporate waffle or big words and complex explanations in an attempt to "soften" or disguise the challenges of the change – even if the official organisation line is written like that. Anyone can make something complicated, there's no skill in that. As Einstein said, "The definition of genius is taking the complex and making it simple." Ask yourself, how would I explain this to a 10-year-old child or a mate at a barbecue on a Sunday afternoon? It's not about dumbing it down or being patronising, it's about using the simplest words you can to ensure the message is clear.

To test your messaging, try it out on your partner or someone who doesn't work for your company (if you can do so without breaking confidentiality) and get them to ask you "what does that mean?" anytime you say something they don't understand. Keep simplifying your message until they get it.

Here are some examples of translating jargon to plain speak:

JARGON	PLAIN SPEAK
"It's about creating synergies between our departments."	"It's about improving the way our departments collaborate and work together."
"It's about the sustainability of our organisation."	"We have to be profitable to survive."
"We have to rationalise our business and this involves rectifying workplace imbalances by refocussing the company's skill set and derecruiting resources."	"We have to make tough decisions to remain in business. That includes reducing the number of staff and making sure those who are here have the right skill set. Unfortunately there will be 10 redundancies."

There may be good reasons – legal reasons – why your company's communication is full of jargon. But let's face it, sometimes the official line is so manufactured, overcooked, highly spun and, for want of a better term, "wanky" that it doesn't even make sense. Your job is to be the sense maker for your team by providing clarity with simplicity.

If you get pushback from above about the way you present the information to your people, confirm you have retained the accuracy of the message, and then be firm and clear about why you're taking this approach: *"My aim is to create clarity for my team. I am not changing the message. I am delivering it in a way my people will hear by making it simple. Communication is only effective if the message is heard and understood."*

TELL STORIES

Use storytelling to connect with people's emotions. As the old sales adage goes, "facts tell, stories sell". Look for opportunities to use a story (it has to be real, not a fabrication) to emphasise why the change is important. For example, if you know your organisation is facing closure and you're trying to rally your people to work right up until the very end and bow out with pride, you may use the closure of Holden or Ford car production in Australia as an example of where this was done well. These two organisations drew on the history of the industry and their companies, plus nostalgia and pride workers had, to ensure people stayed the course and worked hard up until the end.

OWN THE MESSAGE

Debate in private, unite in public.

Although I'm encouraging you to tweak your organisation's message to ensure it is clear and connects with your people, what I'm not doing is giving you permission to diss or publicly criticise the change.

As a leader, you have a responsibility to own your company's message – at least publicly. That doesn't mean you have to lie or overplay it, gushing about how good the change will be to your team when in reality you think it's total rubbish. Remember, people can spot a fake a mile away and this will kill trust. It simply means sticking to the company line without blaming the decision on others, and delivering the information without bagging the change out or sharing too much of your personal opinion.

The time for debating the change and raising your concerns is behind closed doors. Absolutely go hard advocating for your team or against a change if you think it's a bad idea, but be sure to do this in the appropriate forum and in an appropriate way.

Robust conversation in the privacy of your leadership team meeting may be entirely appropriate, but once the decision is made and you leave that room, your job is to own the message, implement the change and lead your people through it.

Don't gossip about who voted for what or voiced which opinion. Don't blame "them" and separate yourself from the rest of the leadership team. This is a time when unity is crucial: "The leadership has decided…" not "they decided".

If you don't like the change or don't have all the information about how the change will impact your people, the temptation can be to avoid any responsibility for delivering the message and instead leave it up to senior management or the communications team to be the messenger. This is a mistake. When you distance yourself from the message, put responsibility for delivering it onto someone else, or blame others for the change decision, it puts you in no-man's land. You're not in the leaders' camp but you're still suspicious in the eyes of your team. You risk losing respect for your leadership from those above and below you. Not only may you be perceived as weak or absent, but also your refusal to own the message gives tacit permission to your people to disengage from the change, making it very hard for you to then rally them behind it.

It's even harder to convince your people to adopt a change if you have outright expressed your disagreement with the change to your people, then need to convince them to adopt it.

Chris, an operations leader, found himself in a difficult position after he openly opposed his company's decision to hire trainees for roles he believed needed skilled and experienced operators.

Chris's concerns were valid and he did try to influence management to have the positions changed to a higher pay grade to attract people with industry experience, but was told that a skills shortage meant trainees were the organisation's best hope. Chris was convinced this was the wrong approach. He had three team members about to retire in the next 18 months and even if the trainees learned fast, they wouldn't be able to fill this knowledge and skill hole. In Chris's mind, the organisation was setting his team and his leadership up for failure. But rather than continue to advocate and use his influencing skills to make his case, Chris got angry. He vented and ranted to his team about what a mistake hiring three new trainees would be. In his anger, he told his staff: "Well, management will soon find out what a mistake they've made when these trainees don't know what they're doing because the rest of us are too busy to teach them. Maybe when this whole idea fails they'll finally get the message that we need experienced people, not kids we need to babysit."

You can probably guess what happened.

When the new trainees were hired, Chris found himself struggling to undo his negative messaging and convince his team to share knowledge and mentor the new starters. His team, having taken Chris's many rants to heart, saw it as their role to prove Chris right and senior management wrong by setting the trainees up for failure.

It was a train wreck, but not for the reasons Chris anticipated. Rather, his lack of leadership and failure to own the message in front of his team created an environment where the trainees could never succeed. It was grossly unfair to the young people who took on these roles with enthusiasm and good intentions that were quickly extinguished. It also exacerbated the skills shortage in the team and caused the team's culture to plummet. This in turn impacted Chris's own performance and reputation as a leader.

The change itself wasn't the problem, Chris's poor leadership was.

Disagreeing with the change publicly may put you "in" with your team but it is negating your leadership responsibility. In extreme cases, it may be seen as outright dissent and your leadership position may be taken away from you. This came very close to happening with Chris.

Remember, your role as a leader is to straddle the needs of the company and the needs of your people.

You have a responsibility to communicate the change and a responsibility to your people to show them that regardless of whether it is seen as a good or bad thing, you are there to lead them through it. You have to accept the change is actually happening – whether you like it or not.

If you don't feel like you have the information you need to be able to own the message and communicate the change, you need to influence up. Speak to your manager or submit a question to the executive team.

And if you really disagree with the change or message? This is where you have a choice. If the change is so far out of alignment with your personal values or morals that you are not ok having anything to do with it, and you've tried to influence up the chain but had no success, it may be time for you to proactively exit the organisation. Leave now before you get caught being unfaithful to who you are as a person. If you choose to stay, remember that your role is to lead your people through the change in the best way you can. Don't get bogged down in what you can't control. Focus on what you can influence. You have the power to support and guide your team through turbulent times by leading them courageously and helping them through – even if you don't like the change that is happening.

BE CLEAR ABOUT WHAT PEOPLE CAN AND CAN'T INFLUENCE

Speaking about what you can influence, it is crucial that you are honest about what, if anything, your people can influence when it comes to the change being made.

Some leaders try to soften their message by telling staff they will consult with them and take their feedback on board when that's not what they intend to do at all.

Do not, I repeat, DO NOT give your people false hope or expectation that their input or feedback can alter the change that is happening if it cannot.

When Bryce's department was about to be restructured, he asked his team for feedback on the new model. The problem was the restructure model had already been decided and the feedback of staff was never going to influence that. But that's not what Bryce said to his people. He gave them false hope and so they invested their time providing ideas and suggestions about how the restructure could look different. They made proposals and held meetings and discussions. They were genuinely trying to help the organisation, and their department, make a better decision. But the decision had been already made. When the staff realised this, and that all their ideas and contributions were futile, they were furious.

What Bryce should have done is have the courage to share the new structure with his team and be clear about what feedback he was asking for and how – if at all – it would be used to influence outcomes. For example, he might have said (after explaining the why and context): *"This is the new structure of our department. While the decision has been made and this structure is what we're going with, I am seeking your feedback on how we can best transition to it."* In this example, the leader is being clear and transparent about what is and isn't on the table for discussion. While your people may not like that they haven't been consulted on the restructure model itself, it's better that you own that than be dishonest or deliberately vague about the role they can play.

When I shared this story with industrial leaders from a large organisation in a workshop in early 2022, it was clear that I had hit a nerve. At one table a group of six leaders were in hushed discussion. I asked if they wanted to share their conversation with the group. One spoke up: "You pretty much just described exactly what has happened in our department in the last few months," he said. "We're going through a restructure and we were told that management was going to 'consult' with us about it. We thought that meant we could influence the change and they didn't say anything to correct that. So, we invested our time providing feedback only to discover that it was for nothing. The new structure had already been decided and they didn't listen to a word we said. It was a total waste of our time and a total lie that we were sold."

The damage this false "consultation" did to the trust these people had for the leader was enormous and the team was now collectively resistant to the change.

GIVE THEM OPTIONS: PEOPLE DON'T LIKE BEING TOLD WHAT TO DO

While your change decision may have already been made and your people may not get a choice about whether it's implemented or not (and being honest about that is vital), if you can give your people options or choice in some part of the decision or how it's rolled out, you will likely see better results.

This idea of giving people a menu to choose from comes from Jonah Berger in his book *The Catalyst*, and is reinforced in Tanya Heaney-Voogt's book *Transforming Norm*.

Heaney-Voogt writes that giving people a menu of options, even if only on small aspects of change, gives people a sense of control – and at an uncertain time that sense can be the difference between people resisting the change and adapting to it.

The menu has to be genuine and provide real choice but, as the leader, it is important that you clearly communicate the parameters in which the menu sits.

For example, harking back to the story in Chapter 2 about the school staff having to change staffrooms on the last day of term, the options presented by the principal could have been:

"We need to move staffrooms so that renovations can take place. Would you prefer to do that:

- ▶ Today before we break for holidays so it's all ready to go when you come back.
- ▶ Over the holidays, understanding that this will be in your personal time.
- ▶ On day one of term four which has been set aside as a student-free day."

If the principal had given her staff options from which they could choose (and some notice!), she would have likely avoided the blow-up that followed when she told staff they had to move.

Consider what menu of options you could give your people as part of your messaging about the change that needs to take place.

SUMMARY

This chapter has been all about providing clarity when courageously communicating change to your team. I've given you a suite of practical strategies to help you convey your message in a considered and transparent way.

Although we've covered a lot of ground, it is important to note this is only a snapshot of the key points to consider when communicating change. I could easily write a whole book on this chapter alone (and may do this in the future).

They key point I want you to take away is this: clear is kind.

- Leaving your people to sit in uncertainty for longer than they need to is cruel.
- Avoiding the difficult conversation because you're afraid of the blow-up is weak.
- Passing the buck to someone else to deliver your message is shirking your responsibility as a leader.

Although these approaches can be tempting and feel like the easier road in the moment, all they do is heighten the temperature of negative emotions and response down the track. Rather than make leading through change smoother, they simply delay the challenge and make your future job so much harder.

So stop being vague about the change and start being clear. Be brave. Show up. Stand up. Do the thinking first and consider your audience. Ask yourself the "who, what, why, when, where and how" questions. Provide the context.

Getting your initial messaging right is the first step. But we don't want to leave it here as a "tell" and consider our work leading people through change as done. Creating clarity is just the beginning. Now it's time to connect with your people – to listen, empathise, get curious and seek their input and opinions. Now it's time to ask and engage.

Chapter 6

CONNECT WITH CURIOSITY

The Five Cs

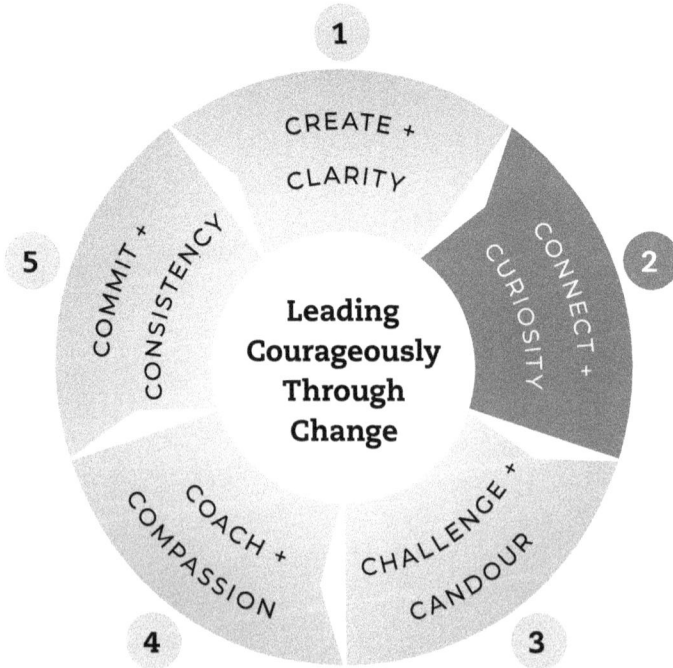

Connect: "To establish communication between."
– Macquarie Dictionary

Curiosity: "The desire to learn or know about anything; inquisitiveness." *– Macquarie Dictionary*

Curiosity is a leadership superpower. It is one of the most important communication tools you have at your disposal. Put simply, the better you know and understand your people, and yourself, the better you can lead them.

Once you've created clarity about the change and explained why it's needed, it's time to step back and create space to listen. Really listen.

When you ask more questions, empathise with others and show them you genuinely care, you supercharge the strength of your relationships and the respect people have for you as a leader.

You also draw out the insights, concerns, feelings and knowledge of your people that will help you lead them through change in a way they want to follow. Get curious about the responses of your people and how they are travelling and you'll be far less likely to be shocked by reactions, resignations and issues with the change you never knew existed, until they blow up. If you don't explore how your people are feeling, even a simple change can suddenly become a big problem that is hard to navigate and implement.

Curiosity isn't just key for leading through change, it is essential for effective communication in any situation, as well as your own personal growth. It's one of the most important "soft" or "human" skills to develop.

When you're curious you're open to learning and new ideas. You're receptive to change and focussed on getting the best outcome rather than being "right".

A curious communicator seeks to understand other perspectives (even if you disagree with them) and welcomes diversity of opinion. You consider why your people are reacting the way they are and dig deeper to uncover their emotions, feelings, fears and concerns. This will help you respond calmly rather than react emotionally under pressure: you get curious, not furious.

Curiosity can be hard. When you feel threatened or under pressure leading change it's easy to adopt a closed mindset without even realising it. Your defences go up and you can find yourself on guard against perceived attacks, reacting based on assumptions without knowing the full picture. You may struggle to listen and instead interject without considering what the other person is really saying. You have a fixed view of how things are done and resist different perspectives.

This armoured response when you are in a closed mindset makes the ability to self-reflect almost impossible. Why self-reflect when you're right and others are wrong? Surely other people are the problem, not you.

Curiosity is not just something you do for other people. It's also something you need to do for yourself. To be able to lead effectively through change, you need to get curious about your own response. You need to reflect on how the change is impacting you and be aware of your own behaviour, actions and communication. Rather than beat yourself up when you get it wrong, you need to look for the learnings and what you could do differently next time.

Closed versus curious mindset

Closed	Curious
No self-reflection	Self-reflects
Oblivious	Self-aware
Wants to be right	Wants to get it right
Defensive	Receptive
Judgmental	Welcomes diversity
Reacts	Responds
Fixed view of world	Open to new ideas
Assumes	Asks
Knows it all	Always learning
Feedback is an attack	Feedback is information

Curiosity takes courage. It requires vulnerability and a willingness to admit you don't know it all or have all the answers about a change.

It also requires psychological safety, that is, an environment where you feel included, safe to learn, safe to contribute, and safe to challenge the status quo without fear of being embarrassed, marginalised or punished in some way (to paraphrase Timothy R Clark in *The 4 Stages of Psychological Safety*). After all, it's much harder to be curious if you're worried about being humiliated for speaking up, belittled for asking questions, or punished for making mistakes.

Asking questions about people's feelings and expecting them to answer truthfully requires trust and vulnerability. If you don't have this relationship with your team already, you'll have to work extra hard to build it now. That's why getting in early before you have to lead through change (as outlined in Chapter 4) is so important. People will not speak up if they don't feel safe to do so.

So how can you be more curious and how, as a leader, can you foster an environment that encourages curiosity as you navigate change? Here are some tips:

1. Ask more questions – of yourself and others.

2. Create a habit of daily self-reflection – what did you do well, what could you improve?

3. Seek to understand, not to respond – clarify what someone else has said to ensure your perception is in line with their intention, rather than making assumptions.

4. Take a deep breath. As listening expert Oscar Trimboli says – the deeper you breathe, the deeper you listen. Pausing between your reaction and response will give you space for curiosity.

5. Welcome feedback about the change and your leadership through it, even if it's difficult to hear.

6. Encourage questions and respond positively when you receive them.

7. Look for learnings rather than blaming or shaming people for mistakes.

8. Shut down people who criticise others for sharing their ideas.

If you don't ask questions, if you don't put yourself in the shoes of your people and consider how they feel about the change, and if you don't show them that you really do care about their response, then expect to lose them, particularly if the change is unpopular. Many people will disengage and feel disempowered. Some may leave your organisation altogether, which can be a huge financial and productivity cost. With skills shortages in many industries across the world, never has people-centred, curious and connected leadership been more important and valuable.

In this chapter I'm going to show you how to supercharge your curiosity to create connection with your team as you lead through change. To do that, you need to be prepared to step up your leadership. You need to be genuine. You need to care. You need to be vulnerable yourself if you expect your people to answer your questions. You need to listen. And if you do, I promise, it will be worth it.

GET CURIOUS WITH YOURSELF

But first thing's first. Before you get curious and ask questions of the people in your team, you need to get curious with yourself.

In the last chapter I asked you to get clear on how you want to show up and lead through the change. Now, I want you to get curious – and brutally honest – about the reality of how you are showing up.

You know how you want to lead and communicate through change but are you doing it? Are you acting in line with what you said? Are you modelling the behaviour you want to see in others?

If you don't get curious about your own response and behaviour, it's really easy for the clarity you came to in Chapter 5 to be irrelevant. That clarity about how you want to show up means nothing if you don't do it.

Now is the time for more honest self-reflection. That's my polite way of asking you to please not bullshit yourself, because humans are good at that. We tell ourselves stories to justify our own behaviour. We make excuses. We deny, blame others, justify and defend. We build barriers around us. I'm asking you to put all of those down. It's a big ask, I know. And to be frank – there's a chance you may not be up to the challenge. You'll be tempted to skip over this and tell yourself "I'm fine" when the reality may be far from it. My challenge to you now is to go there. Ask yourself the tough questions and answer them as honestly as you can. You can't change what you don't acknowledge and you can't lead effectively if you're behaving in ways that create disconnection with your team.

CURIOUS QUESTIONS TO REFLECT ON

Below are just some of the questions you could reflect on before you get curious with your team. Note: this isn't about self-indulgent navel gazing, beating yourself up or self-loathing, it's about getting really honest and curious with yourself so you're in the best working order to connect with curiosity with your team. Self-reflection in order to build your self-awareness is something the best leaders do.

- If I had to describe how I'm feeling about the change using two words, what would they be?
- How am I travelling right now, really?
- Is my mindset about this change, my people's reactions and my own leadership closed or curious?
- Am I modelling the behaviour I want to see in others?
- Am I regularly reflecting on my mindset, actions, behaviour and how I show up for my team?
- Am I regulating my emotions to ensure I express them appropriately?
- Am I open to and welcoming feedback?
- Are there conversations I'm avoiding?
- What am I doing well as a leader?
- What do I need to improve?
- How do I respond when one of my team resists the change? Why do I react that way?
- What emotions do I struggle with myself and in other people, and why is that?
- Am I focussed on getting the best outcome or am I focussed on being right?
- Am I receptive to new ideas from my team or am I defensive?
- Am I leading in a way that I would want to follow if I was a member of my team?

EMPATHY IS ESSENTIAL

If you want to connect with your people and show them you care, while also increasing your understanding of how they are responding to a change, empathy is essential.

In fact, it's often described as the top trust-building tool we have and one of the core leadership skills to develop.

Why? Because it allows people to feel cared for, seen and heard – and everyone wants that.

What is empathy?

Empathy is listening to someone else's experience and believing them. You don't have to have had that experience yourself, you don't have to like or agree with their description of how they feel, but you do have to believe it is what the experience or feeling is for them.

> Empathy is curiosity in action. It's seeking to understand, not to respond. It's putting yourself in another person's shoes and seeing things from their perspective, even if you disagree.

Empathy is different to sympathy. Sympathy is feeling sorry for someone. Empathy is feeling with someone. It's connecting to the emotions someone is experiencing, even if you can't connect with the circumstances or the behaviour. You might think someone's angry reaction to a relatively minor change is over the top but empathy allows you to consider a time when you have been angry, connect with what it feels like to be in that space, and then relate to the other person in a more considered way. Empathy is acknowledging, not dismissing these feelings. For example:

"I can see you're really upset." "I appreciate this is frustrating." "I want to acknowledge that some of you are really angry."

Empathy is listening without judgement, then clarifying and repeating what you hear. *"So what I'm hearing you say is that you're really hurt and upset that there was no consultation about this change before it was announced. Would you say that's right?"*

What empathy is:

- Connecting with the emotions someone is experiencing.
- Sitting with someone in the dark, without trying to fix it.
- Getting curious, not furious: *"I noticed a change in your behaviour and I wanted to check in – are you ok?"* or *"Tell me more about…"*
- Seeking to understand, not to respond. *"So what I'm hearing is…Have I got that right?"*
- Using "I" statements so they feel heard.

What empathy is not:

- Solving the problem.
- One-upmanship.
- Saying "I know how you feel…"
- Moving on because the emotions are uncomfortable.
- Conceding or excusing poor behaviour because you feel sorry for them.

Empathy is a great tool for helping you to regulate your own emotions under pressure. Instead of simply reacting and wishing the person would "just get on with it", putting yourself in the other person's shoes will help you try to understand where they're coming from. You may still disagree with their response. You may still think that their reaction is over the top or that they're being unreasonable, but rather than judge their reaction through your own lens, you pause and try to imagine what's going on for them and see it through their eyes instead.

Empathy allows you to recognise the humanity in another person and realise that although there may be differences between you, they are just like you. They are trying to navigate this change just like you. They care about their work just like you. They want to support their family just like you. They get nervous about challenge, change and uncertainty, just like you. They may be responding differently to how you would, but they are human too.

Empathising and putting himself in the shoes of his staff was at the core of Andy McCarthy's leadership through change when he led the acquisition of multiple solar businesses under the RACV Solar banner in his time as CEO.

"When we acquired the business in Bendigo one of the first things I did was sit down and look at the organisation chart of the company we were acquiring," Andy said.

"Rather than look at them as names on a piece of paper, I thought about the people behind the names. I considered what their worlds looked like. I wondered: What's their history? Why do they work for that company? What motivates them every day? What do they love about what they do? What do they hate about it? And what is this change going to do to this particular person in isolation?

"As a business grows there can be a tendency to look at your workforce as a bunch of names on the payroll. But I always try and remember that it's 170 people, 170 stories, and they've all got hopes and dreams and anxieties and passion, and they're all making personal sacrifice for their professional careers.

"When you start to look at each person as an individual then your understanding of the human element of what you're doing becomes really, really clear. You have to start with people first and until you understand the impact on people and how to lead that, you can't do the other pieces of work. If the people don't come with you through the change, the change won't be successful."

EMPATHY AS A TOOL FOR DE-ESCALATING CONFLICT

Not only is empathy a key trust-building tool, it's also a brilliant strategy for de-escalating anger, aggression and conflict – all of which can be prevalent at times of change, particularly if the change is unpopular. It's my go-to strategy when I'm facilitating volatile or hostile meetings.

Many years ago I was the communications manager for a water corporation that was building a $200 million world-first wastewater treatment and recycling system in Gippsland. The project was partially funded through water tariffs and contributed to residential water bills doubling over five years. Although it was a vital project that had many benefits for the community, because of the cost and the encroachment of pipes through farmland, it was not popular with everyone.

One community meeting in particular stands out. It was with affected landholders who were particularly heated. The anger was palpable before the meeting even started. You could feel the tension in the room and see that people were on edge. So, the first thing the facilitator did when they walked out in front of that room full of people was empathise and acknowledge the emotion by saying something like this:

"Ok folks, we are here tonight to discuss this project but before we do, I want to acknowledge that there's a lot of feeling in the room tonight. Some of you are angry, concerned and upset, and that's ok. I'm here to hear about those concerns and hopefully allay them. But for us to be able to have this discussion what I ask of you is that we treat each other with respect. And what respect looks like to me is:

- *If you've got a question please pop your hand up.*

- *There's no need for us to yell or swear at each other, so let's keep it polite.*

- *I want to hear from everyone in the room so if you ask a question I'll then go to anyone else in the room who wants to speak before coming back to you for another go.*

"Again, I appreciate there are strong feelings in the room but that doesn't mean we can't have this conversation in a constructive and positive way."

Something powerful happens in a room when you address the elephant and acknowledge the emotion by empathising upfront. You can see people de-escalate in front of your eyes. They don't have to keep showing you they're angry because you've acknowledged that they are, so they're more likely to soften and engage in the conversation.

This strategy of coupling empathy with some basic ground rules is a great way to keep fiery meetings under control.

I've also seen leaders approach meetings like this in a very different way. When they see that the crowd is angry, rather than empathise, they armour up. It's as if they're going into battle and they stride out onto stage and launch straight into the facts of the project, completely ignoring the emotion in the room. And here's what happens: the anger rises. Because the speaker hasn't acknowledged people's feelings, they feel the need to show it and things get out of control very fast. Someone yells out, "What's the point?" Another follows up with, "This is rubbish!" And before long you've got multiple people shouting and heckling as the speaker tries to keep things on track. The speaker ends up playing a version of whack-a-mole, trying to tell people to calm down and behave, only to have another person escalate.

Ignoring the feeling in the room doesn't make it go away, it just makes it grow. If you want to have a chance of connecting with your audience and actually having a conversation about the change in a respectful, constructive and appropriate way, empathy is the secret sauce that will help you do that.

INJECTING EMPATHY IS SIMPLE BUT INCREDIBLY POWERFUL

Injecting empathy into one-on-one or group conversations during change is important whether the other person is obviously angry and upset, or not. It's about connection and showing you care. It's easy to do too and doesn't take much time or effort at all, just a little bit of conscious thought.

Shane was a senior leader at a manufacturing company who was overseeing an unpopular site-wide restructure instigated by a new CEO. I asked Shane what he was saying to his people when they quizzed him for more information about the changes. Shane's response? "I just tell them to stay focussed on doing their job safely and to not be distracted by the uncertainty going on around us."

I suggested that while his message wasn't necessarily wrong, it lacked empathy, understanding and acknowledgement that people were going through a really challenging time. I suggested that he make a slight tweak to his message: instead of jumping straight into, "We need to continue to focus on safety and get the job done", I encouraged him to start with something like this:

"I appreciate that this is a challenging time, that uncertainty is unnerving and change is hard. I don't have any more information that I can share with you at the moment but my commitment to you is to communicate any detail I have as soon as I have it. In the meantime, we need to make sure that we continue to focus on doing our jobs safely, because the last thing we want is for someone to get hurt because they're distracted."

What you can see here is the addition of empathy. It's still Shane's clear, plain, direct message, but with some warmth injected as well, which will give his message more chance of being heard.

GET CURIOUS NOT FURIOUS

The more you can understand your team's fears, concerns and frustrations about a change, the better you can address them.

Leading through change is often high pressure. It's easy to be reactive and get furious when you're stressed and your people are stressed. It's a simple fact that when you are not at your best, your communication is not at its best. But a common mistake by leaders in these moments is to shut down debate, or react angrily because your people are angry. As we discussed earlier, your communication and mood are contagious and it's really easy to get sucked in.

That's why one of the most useful responses in these times of pressure and stress is this: get curious not furious. This became my mantra during COVID, particularly when engaging in conversations with people who had opinions and beliefs that were the polar opposite to me. "Get curious not furious, Leah," I would urge myself silently. "Get curious not furious."

What did this then look like in practice? Rather than jumping down someone's throat and saying something unhelpful and inflammatory like: "You're being ridiculous!" (as tempting as it was) I would ask a question instead.

For example:

- *"That's really different to how I see things. Can you tell me how you came to that position?"*

- *"I want to try to understand where you're coming from. What specifically about the change is it that you don't like?"*

- *"I want to make sure I'm clear here. Can you tell me more about why you feel that way?"*

- *"I can see you're upset. Can you help me understand why you're reacting so strongly to this?"*

Reacting with genuine curiosity rather than defensiveness or anger when I disagreed with someone helped me do five important things in the heat of the moment:

1. Put a pause between my reaction and response, allowing me to regulate my emotions. Asking a question created the space I needed to take a few deep breaths and calm down.

2. Get the context I needed to more clearly understand where the other person was coming from. I may have been ready to bite the person's head off for their position, only to discover they'd had an experience in their past that explained why they felt that way. I may still have disagreed with them, but I could understand how they got there.

3. Ensure the other person felt listened to. Let's face it, we all want to feel understood, seen and heard. Asking a question before you jump in with your response shows you actually care about where they're coming from.

4. Provide a more considered response. I could adjust my reply based on the additional information that asking a question elicited. For example: *"Thank you for sharing that. I appreciate that may have been your experience, but from my position I think..."*

5. Increase my chances of the other person listening to me because I had first taken the time to listen to them. The other person may not like or agree with what you have to say, but they will be more inclined to listen to you if you've listened to them.

Even if the end result was still that we totally disagreed with each other, rather than escalate immediately to an argument, getting curious not furious ensured we were more likely to enter into a considered disagreement or debate about ideas, not each other.

Curious not furious was a gamechanger for Clare, a leader I worked with over a 12-month period. Clare realised she was going into every meeting with a particular group of colleagues with an antagonistic mindset. She was in fight mode before a word had even been spoken. No wonder the meetings always went pear-shaped quickly – she was showing up already in battle. When she acknowledged that she was being furious, not curious, Clare was able to do something about it. She scheduled five-to-ten minutes before these meetings to centre and calm herself, and carried the mantras of "assume positive intent" and "get curious not furious" into each conversation. Of course, some meetings still ended in hostility, but far less than had before.

ACTION

Practice responding with curiosity rather than defensiveness or anger the next time you disagree with someone. Rather than listening to respond or interrupting, try responding with:

"Tell me more…"

"Can you share with me how you came to that position?" or

"Help me understand where you're coming from…"

CURIOSITY IN PRACTICE

If curiosity and asking questions in this style is new for you and your team, you may need to articulate what you're doing first so people are not suspicious. For example, you could say: *"I know I haven't been great at asking questions of you in the past but I'm looking to change that now. Getting an understanding of your thoughts and feelings is important."*

This is where the Q&A sparring activity outlined in Chapter 5 can again be helpful. Put yourself in your team's position and pre-empt some of the questions they are likely to ask. That way you'll be better prepared with a response.

Depending on your team, curious questions may or may not be posed in a group environment. Only you will know what is likely to work best. If possible, connecting in a group environment (if it's psychologically and physically safe to do so) to discuss the change is often valuable as everyone hears the same information and answers at the same time, which often minimises the need for you to repeatedly answer the same questions in one-on-one conversations.

If you do want to get curious with your team as a group, here are four approaches to consider:

1. You pose an open-ended question that gives direction to the group and have a normal, free-flowing discussion. For tips on how to manage this and ensure it doesn't get out of hand, see "Managing the Angry Mob" coming up in the next chapter.

2. Put the people in your team into small group discussions of two to four people for 10 to 15 minutes and ask them to share how they feel about the change with each other and the questions they'd like answered. Get the group to collate their questions and have one member report back on the overall feelings and pose the questions.

3. Give everyone a sticky note and a pen and ask them to write down one to three questions they have about the change (or use one of the questions outlined on the upcoming pages). Collect the sticky notes and stick them to a whiteboard or flipchart. Group similar questions together and then answer them. If you are confident enough to do this on the spot, go for it! Any you can't answer you can always take on notice and come back with an answer to later.

   Or you may like to collect the sticky notes, go away and review them, work out your answers and schedule a follow up session for a few days' or a week's time. Make sure you communicate clearly with your team how and when you will follow up.

By getting people to write their questions on sticky notes and making it clear they will NOT have to share in front of the group, you are likely to get honest responses. This also helps to cut out "group think" where everyone agrees with the dominant voice just to keep the peace.

4. Use online software like Mentimeter to boost engagement and collect anonymous feedback in real time by running polls and collecting answers to questions through people's individual mobile phones. You can build immediate connection with your audience and make them part of your presentation, allowing them to vote, ask questions and interact throughout. I've used this platform in many strategic planning sessions with great success. Welcome the feedback.

ASK GREAT QUESTIONS (NOTE: "ANY QUESTIONS?" IS NOT ONE OF THEM)

Greg stood in front of his department after finishing a presentation on the new redundancy and restructure program that would be introduced in the coming months in a bid to reduce the workforce by 20 per cent.

"Any questions?" he asked, looking around the sea of 100+ faces.

No one put their hand up. No one answered.

"None at all?" Greg prompted. "I'm happy to answer them."

Still nothing. Crickets chirping. They gave him silence.

Of course, the lack of questions asked of Greg publicly in

this forum did not mean there were no questions. Everyone had questions but they were too afraid, insecure, worried or nervous to ask them in a group environment when it was an open floor "any questions" situation.

The risk here was that Greg walked away thinking, "Job done. I asked if anyone had questions, I gave them the opportunity to ask them, and they didn't. So either there are no questions or it's their fault for not asking them."

Now, there were likely lots of things going on in this situation – a lack of psychological safety in the room being one of them. But the generic framing of Greg's "any questions?" question was also part of the problem.

Was he really open to ANY questions? Because his question was so broad and generic, people did not feel brave enough to ask anything. What if they asked the "wrong" question? Then what? There was too much risk.

The quality of the feedback you receive directly corresponds with the quality of the questions you ask.

My advice here? Ask open-ended questions with direction. Make them broad enough to encourage a variety of answers, but specific enough to give people something to work with.

Here are some examples of open-ended questions you may want to ask your team as you navigate change:

- ► Based on the information I've given you, what's the number one question you have?
- ► How can we best implement the change?
- ► What would successfully navigating this change look like to you?

- ▸ What support do you need to succeed?

- ▸ What do you need from me?

- ▸ How can I help?

- ▸ What else do you want to know?

- ▸ What's your biggest concern about the change?

- ▸ What is something we may not have considered that you want us to keep front of mind when we're implementing this change?

- ▸ What questions do you still have that we haven't answered and you're likely to ask each other about when you walk away from this meeting?

- ▸ What was your key takeaway from that update?

- ▸ What questions would you like me to try to get answered for you?

CURIOSITY REQUIRES THE COURAGE TO ACCEPT FEEDBACK WELL

Connecting with curiosity only works if you're able to receive the feedback you get in a calm and considered way. Feedback is not a dirty word. Feedback gives you the gift of insight. I encourage you to seek it from your team during times of change and welcome it when it's forthcoming. If you don't actively welcome and encourage feedback you are unlikely to receive it. This can mean you miss out on vital information to help you navigate the change effectively. Sure, you might not like what you hear but when you have insight into how your people are feeling, you can be a better leader.

I will outline a basic framework for receiving feedback in a moment, but before I do, a reminder from Chapter 5 to be very clear on what feedback you're actually seeking. I've said it before but I'll say it again: do not suggest your people can influence the change if they can't.

Eight tips for receiving feedback well:

1. Seek first to understand, then to respond

Very few of us truly listen when another person is talking. Instead, we half-listen to what the person is saying and use the rest of our brain to focus on formulating our response.

The result? We don't really hear what the person is trying to tell us because we're too busy focussed on our comeback.

Instead, focus on listening to understand the other person's point of view.

2. Drop the defence and assume positive intent

Most people give feedback with good intentions, so drop the immediate defensive response. Be open to hearing what the person has to say. Instead of viewing their feedback as an attack, see it as an opportunity to learn, understand your people better, and make improvements to the change or how you implement it if you can.

This can be tough. It's easy to react defensively and become aggressive when someone asks a question or makes a statement that we're sure has an underlying meaning. Our assumption can be "they're out to get us" so we go on the attack. Fight against that response. Instead of assuming negative intent, assume instead that their intent for raising their concerns with you is positive and be open to listening.

Note: This does not mean you have to agree with the feedback the other person gives you. In fact, be absolutely prepared to say you disagree and why. But be open to receiving the feedback in the first place.

3. Drill down

Help the person drill down to pinpoint their specific concern rather than speak in generalisations like saying "the whole thing is crap".

Ask questions about how the person came to their point of view. If someone thinks you're leading the change badly, ask them why. You need more information. What is it about your behaviour that made them come to that conclusion? Why do they think like that? Is their feedback grounded in fact and reality, or have they made assumptions about you?

4. Seek specific examples

Just like it's important to give specific examples when delivering difficult feedback or communicating a change message, it's also important to ask for them when you're the one receiving feedback.

If someone thinks the change is going to result in safety risks for the workforce, ask them to give you examples of what these safety risks might be. Of course you want to understand if there are genuine safety risks that may come with the change but you also want to determine that "safety" isn't being used as a decoy. I have seen this happen more than once.

5. Ask questions for clarity and confirm you've understood

Don't assume that just because you've been given an example or detailed explanation that you are on the same page as the other person. It's always important to check this by clarifying or repeating back your take on what the other person has said. This is where you might ask:

"What is the number one thing you want me to take away from this conversation?"

Or say something like:

"So, what I'm hearing you say is…Have I got that right?" or *"Is that what you meant?"*

6. Put a pause between your reaction and your response

If you get angry or upset when confronted with difficult feedback about the change or your leadership, when possible, ask for a break or more time rather than responding in the moment when your emotions are high.

Instead, say something like: *"You've caught me a bit off guard. Can you leave that with me for half an hour* [or a few minutes – whatever timeframe you need] *so I can have a think about it and get back to you?"*

If you are feeling defensive you may consider even saying that outright. For example: *"I'm feeling defensive right now and I'm not sure I'm in the best space to take this all in. Can you let me consider that and we'll talk it through tomorrow?"*

Then, go away and let your emotions out in private before composing yourself and returning to have the conversation calmly and rationally, making sure you communicate your key messages clearly.

If taking a physical break isn't possible, put a pause between your reaction and response by taking a drink of water or saying something like, *"Let me think about that for a moment,"* or *"I'm just letting that sink in."* Even a few seconds to consider your response may mean you handle the situation better than if you just launched into a reply with your heart and not your head.

7. Look for the learnings

Even if the feedback is hard to hear, it's always worth looking for the learnings. What can you do differently based on the feedback? What gift has the insight given you? Sometimes these "gifts" can be the tough realisation that someone you thought was a person you could trust is not that person at all.

8. Be grateful

Even if you totally disagree with the feedback you've received, be grateful the person gave it to you. No, you don't have to be grateful for what they said, but rather the fact they had the courage to say it to your face rather than behind your back. Knowing how someone perceives you, your actions or a change can be valuable information to have.

Receiving feedback takes practice and you don't get good at what you don't do. The more you practise, the better you get. Also, by modelling receiving feedback well, your people will be more open to taking feedback from you.

SUMMARY

In this chapter we've spoken about the importance of connecting with curiosity, asking questions, empathising and listening.

Connecting with curiosity is essential to leading through change as it builds trust and gives you the gift of insight.

It's important to understand that this is not a one-off set-and-forget conversation. You need to keep circling back, checking in with your people, and asking questions. There will be more on that in Chapter 9 but it's worth mentioning here too.

Use the information in this chapter as the foundation to help you practise curiosity. Change your ask-to-tell ratio and ask more questions.

While this chapter focussed on warmth (which requires vulnerability and courage), in the next chapter we'll explore how to bring strength to your leadership by challenging with candour.

Chapter 7

CHALLENGE WITH CANDOUR

The Five Cs

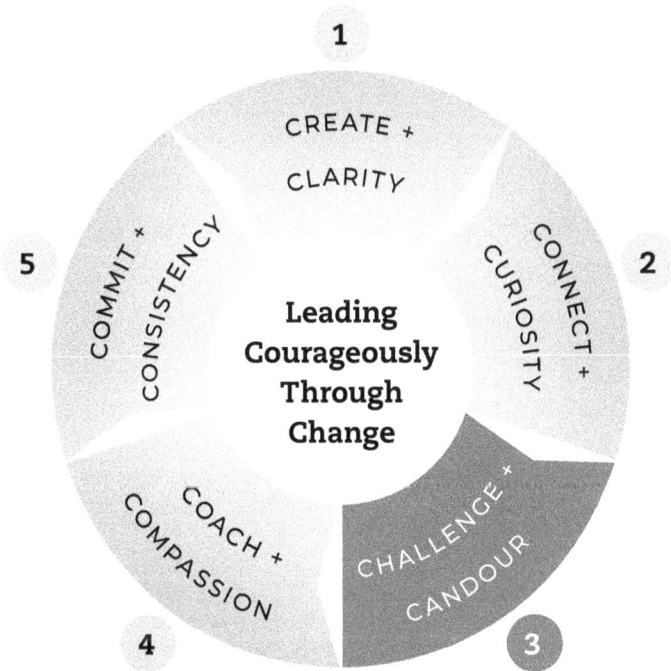

Challenge: "A calling to account or into question"
– *Macquarie Dictionary*

Candour: "Frankness as of speech; sincerity; honesty." – *Macquarie Dictionary*

Navigating change is hard. But in the middle of the hard you have a choice about how you respond. Reminding yourself and your people of this choice requires you to challenge with candour.

Many leaders I work with will be tempted to skip Chapter 6 (Connect with Curiosity) and jump straight from Chapter 5 (Create Clarity) to this chapter on holding people accountable. BUT, crucially, the strategies outlined in this chapter only work effectively if you have led with warmth first.

The empathy and connection piece is key. It builds trust, care and respect. It's only when you have that – and more information about how your people are feeling based on the questions you explored with curiosity – that you can challenge in a frank and firm way without losing people.

This is where you may need to give your people some hard truths. You may need to let them know that they can let change happen to them and sink in the storm, drown or lose their way, or they can steer the ship through the storm in control of their behaviour and actions, even in the face of great challenge.

It's where you challenge the victim mentality and help your team steer towards creating their own future. Where you challenge your own mindset to ensure you're modelling the behaviour required to be resilient and ok with uncertainty.

It's where you have open and honest conversations about what it will take to get through the change in the best way possible. Where you challenge your people to stick with you, and are frank about the consequences if they react poorly or outright resist. It's where you challenge behaviour.

Don't shy away from tough conversations when leading your team through change and certainly don't allow poor behaviour to go unchecked.

Absolutely, empathise with where your people are at and take this into consideration, but even through difficult times you still have a responsibility as a leader to hold your people to account for their performance and behaviour.

If you don't – if you let your people off the hook because dealing with change is hard for everyone – the wheels can fall off for individuals, teams and, in extreme cases, whole organisations as people "give up" or act like it's the Wild West and anything goes. The damage that can be done in these moments of extreme change pressure can be hard – and sometimes impossible – to come back from after the change has passed.

This is also when you may have to challenge up the chain and endeavour to influence your upper management by sharing the impact of the change on your team, and the concerns they have raised with you.

And through it all, regardless of who you are speaking with, you need to stay hard on the issue, soft on the person. Yes, challenge with candour but do not lose that empathy and care.

In short, as a leader, you need to challenge your own and other people's:

- focus
- mindset
- avoidance/unfettered optimism
- behaviour
- group think and the squeaky wheel.

In this chapter I show you how.

CHALLENGE FOCUS

"Where your attention goes, your energy flows." This principle has been attributed to many people over the years and is absolutely applicable here.

Over the years I've worked with many leaders and teams who have wasted incredible amounts of time worrying about things they can't control or influence. They tie themselves in knots worrying about decisions that may or may not be made by the executive, board or government and not only does this not change the situation or circumstance, it feeds their fear and anxiety and makes them feel like crap.

One of the very first things I help them with is learning to control their controllables and let the rest go.

Now, this doesn't mean that people in the team are not allowed to express their dissatisfaction with a change but what it does mean is focussing their attention on what will help not hinder the way they cope under pressure. It's helping them to know when they've done all they can, the decision is out of their hands, and they have to accept the change is happening and turn their focus to how they respond.

To do this I draw on Stephen Covey's circles of influence work by getting people to reflect on these three questions:

1. What can I control?
2. What can I influence?
3. What do I need to let go of?

WHAT CAN I CONTROL?

In a nutshell, when it comes to the things you can control during change it's not situation, circumstance or other people – it's you.

You can control you and that's pretty much it.

You can't control what other people do or what they think of you and the change, and you can't control a lot of what goes on around you. But what you can control are the choices you make about how you manage yourself, your emotions, your behaviour, your actions and your communication.

It's important to note, however, that your ability to take control of these things is limited to your AWARENESS about yourself and the actions you take. You won't be able to control your behaviour if you don't realise there's a problem with your behaviour in the first place.

Things you can control as you lead through change are:

▸ Your response to other people, situations and circumstances.

▸ How you express your emotions.

▸ The way you communicate and lead.

▸ Your body language.

▸ Your mood.

▸ Your mindset.

▸ The energy you bring.

▸ The way you take care of yourself with the big basic three: sleep, diet and exercise.

WHAT CAN I INFLUENCE?

While you can't control other people, you can influence them and that influence is based on your understanding of the human condition, making connections, communication and building relationships.

The number one thing you can do to strengthen your influence during change is to build your relationships. If people trust, like and respect you, they will be much more inclined to listen to, believe and follow you as their leader.

While the things you can influence will differ depending on the situation, here are some possibilities:

- ▸ How your people respond to the change message (based on how well you communicate and the relationship you have with them).
- ▸ Whether your people implement the change.
- ▸ The way the change is rolled out (by influencing up).
- ▸ The timing of the change implementation.
- ▸ The way management, government or the relevant decision-maker responds to you team's feedback about the change (based on your communication).
- ▸ What people think of your leadership and how they respond to you.

WHAT DO I NEED TO LET GO OF?

It's natural to worry about the impact of change, even if you can't control or influence it, but focussing too much attention on the situation will only make you feel like rubbish. And while you feel rubbish, the situation and circumstance remain the same. Yes, you are allowed to be sad, scared and angry. Of course you're allowed to grieve and feel your feelings. But eventually you need to let go.

Things you may need to let go of as you lead through change include:

- How other people choose to respond to you and your communication.
- What other people say and do.
- Many of the things that happen to and around you (your situation and circumstance).
- The fact that the change is happening.
- What the change is.

When I introduce this concept of letting go in my workshops, one of the most common questions I get asked is: "But how do I let go of those things I'm worrying about that I can't control and influence? I can't just magically make that disappear." Of course you can't. But what you can do is accept it.

According to Australia's leading mindset coach, Ben Crowe, if you want to be ok with uncertainty, change and the unknown, you need to practise radical acceptance.

"Either you accept the things you can't control or you suffer, it's as simple as that," Crowe, who has been mindset coach to the likes of tennis stars Ash Barty and Dylan Alcott, has said in many interviews.

How can you use the "control, influence, let go" three-question framework to challenge yourself and your team with candour during change?

I encourage you to throw any challenge you have against them. Use them to ensure you are clear on where to best focus your time and energy. Use them to help you understand what you need to let go of.

By helping your team focus on what they can control and influence, you give them a sense power and empowerment at a time when they may otherwise feel powerless.

Some further questions you may like to explore are:

- ▸ What am I spending too much time discussing or worrying about that I can't control or influence and need to let go of?
- ▸ How can I use my influence more effectively?
- ▸ What actions can I take that will help me regulate myself and where can I schedule them in my calendar?

CHALLENGE ETHOS/MINDSETS

Even if your focus is on the things you can control and influence, during a challenging change it is easy to get sucked into a mindset of negativity, or as I like to call it – victim mode. Even people who initially respond well can dip into this mindset. Remember, we don't respond to change in a straight line. If I was really going to capture the trajectory of responses to change I'd probably be best to just scribble all over a page.

This is when you need to challenge your own and other people's thinking. This is when you need to train your brain to choose your response and be a creator of your reality, rather than be a victim to circumstance. Your mindset underpins your ability to self-manage, be resilient, communicate with and lead others effectively during change.

As the saying goes, "Your mind can be your strongest muscle or worst enemy. Train it well."

My favourite models for challenging leaders and teams to reflect on their mindsets under pressure are Stephen Karpman's "Karpman Drama Triangle" and David Emerald's TED* (*The Empowerment Dynamic). These models have underpinned my work for the last 10 years, featured in my first book *Soft is the New Hard*, and are also my go-to when I'm dealing with hardship, change and uncertainty in my own life.

I'm going to outline them below and as you read the descriptions I encourage you to consider which position in the triangles you have been showing up from lately. Are you most often in the Drama Triangle or The Empowerment Dynamic? How about your team? Remember, you can't change what you don't acknowledge, so I encourage you to be brutally honest with yourself. Here goes:

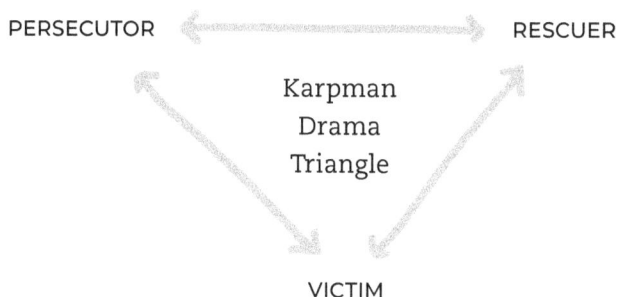

PERSECUTOR ⟷ RESCUER

Karpman
Drama
Triangle

VICTIM

MAKING SHIFTS HAPPEN

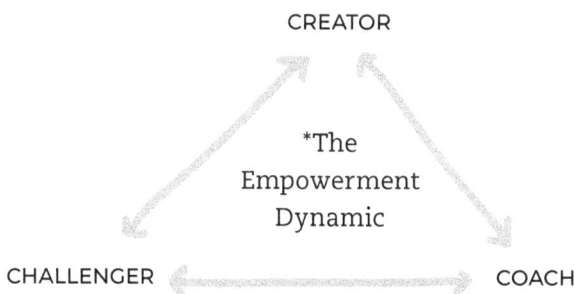

CREATOR

*The
Empowerment
Dynamic

CHALLENGER ⟷ COACH

KARPMAN DRAMA TRIANGLE
(AKA THE DREADED DRAMA TRIANGLE)

Presented as an inverted pyramid, Karpman's Drama Triangle (1968) features three positions – victim, persecutor and rescuer. Karpman suggested many people live their whole lives from a position in the Drama Triangle without even realising it, and it holds them back.

VICTIM MODE

According to Karpman, a victim is someone who focusses on all the problems in their life and the events they don't want to happen – which may include the change you're trying to implement with your team.

Their internal (and often external) narrative goes something like this: "Poor me. Why do bad things always happen to me? Life's not fair." They feel powerless, at the mercy of situation and circumstance, and feel like their dreams are lost and denied.

Just like people who focus too much of their attention on things they can't control or influence, operating from the victim perspective doesn't change a person's situation or circumstance, it just makes them feel like rubbish.

If you or your team go into victim mode during the change, you'll quickly fall into a funk. You'll blame other people for how you're feeling, justify your own poor behaviour and become defensive. You won't take personal responsibility because you believe none of this is your fault. Others have done this to you. You'll lament that the change is happening to you and that it's not fair. And you'll often have no conscious awareness that you're doing it.

If you get a whole team of people fall into victim mode, you're in for a rough ride. When this happens, people come into work only to bitch and whinge about the same grievances and problems day in and day out. They can't see past their own misery and the spiral into toxicity can quickly suck other people in.

PERSECUTOR MODE

Often, people who start out as victims shift to the position of persecutor in the Drama Triangle during change and uncertainty. As with the victim, a persecutor also focusses on problems, blames other people and feels hard done by. But unlike the victim, they get angry. Really angry. They need someone to point the finger at, to shout at and to blame. "This is your fault, your fault and your fault," they yell. They dominate, tear others down and react aggressively.

Although this position is damaging (to both the persecutor themselves and those around them), it can feel powerful, which is often why persecutors continue their destructive behaviour. It also gives them a sense of control and certainty in uncertain times.

During the height of the COVID pandemic, when vaccine mandates and lockdowns were in place, we saw a lot of people shift into persecutor mode. Many people wanted and needed someone to blame.

RESCUER MODE

And then you've got rescuer mode. This is where many leaders I work with – who didn't think they would fit in the Drama Triangle at all – suddenly have the realisation that this is them, particularly when things get tough within their team.

The rescuer is often the people pleaser. The person who tries to save the day, fix the problem, relieve the pain and make everything better. A leader who is a rescuer will be poor at delegating (because it's quicker and easier to just do it yourself) and may see their role as the protector of their people. They are almost always well-intentioned and genuinely believe they are doing the right thing. Some can have a superhero complex and may feel righteous or behave like a bit of a martyr.

While it may sound like a positive thing, the rescuer role creates unintended consequences and often co-dependent relationships with victims. You see, victims are always looking for someone to rescue them, and by carrying out this role and jumping in to "save the day", the rescuer unintentionally keeps the victim in victim mode, rather than encouraging them to help themselves. This often then causes frustration for the rescuer.

I've heard many leaders say, "But why do they keep coming to me to fix all their problems?" The answer I often find myself giving a rescuer? "Because you always fix their problems."

Don't get me wrong, wanting to support, protect, and help your people through change is a wonderful thing. As you know, leading with warmth, empathy and care is a core message in this book. But overstepping the mark and becoming a chronic rescuer is problematic. You can't help someone who won't help themselves. It's one of life's toughest lessons. Your job is to lead yourself and your people through the change in a way that encourages and empowers them to follow. You can't do it for them.

Operating from a position in the Drama Triangles does not make you a bad person or a poor leader. But it will make it difficult for your to communicate and lead effectively through change.

The good news is, there is an alternative.

TED* (*THE EMPOWERMENT DYNAMIC)

American author and co-founder of the Bainbridge Leadership Centre's Centre for The Empowerment Dynamic, David Emerald Womeldorff, outlined this model in his book, *The Power of TED* (*The Empowerment Dynamic)*, first published in 2005 under the pen name David Emerald. In his model, developed as a direct alternative to Karpman's Drama Triangle, Emerald highlighted how a focus on choice and outcomes, rather than problems, could lead to a positive shift in the way a person approached life's challenges.

TED* features an upright triangle with three positions that are mirror alternatives to the Drama Triangle.

BE A CREATOR, NOT A VICTIM

Rather than a victim, TED* features the role of creator – a person who focusses on the outcome they want rather than the problem they face. The person who operates from creator mode is conscious of their power to choose their response and create their own reality, even in the face of great pressure, uncertainty and change. By focussing on outcomes and end goals rather than problems, the creator is able to be resilient through challenging times. They recognise that bad things happen to good people all the time and life is not fair, in fact sometimes it sucks, but rather than let that consume them, they look for ways to deal with it and work through the problems.

The role of creator in TED* builds on the work of Austrian neurologist and psychiatrist, Viktor Frankl. In the 1930s, Frankl was married and had a loving family. Then World War II broke out. During the war, because he was Jewish, Frankl spent three years imprisoned in Nazi ghettos and various concentration camps, including the infamous Auschwitz.

Forced to work as a slave labourer in the depths of winter, starved and witness to some of the most horrific atrocities in human history, Frankl captured his experiences in a book published shortly after the war, which was eventually translated as *Man's Search for Meaning* (1946). The book went on to sell more than 10 million copies worldwide and is credited by many of the most successful business leaders since as being the book that changed their mindset when dealing with the challenges and uncertainty of life.

Amidst the horror of war, in which his wife, father, mother and brother were all killed, Frankl discovered that even in the most brutal of circumstances we all have the power to choose. No matter what, no matter how bad it gets – we always have the power to choose our response.

I shared Frankl's words in *Soft is the New Hard* and I share them again here:

"Everything can be taken from a man but one thing: the last of the human freedoms – to choose one's attitude in any given set of circumstances, to choose one's own way. When we are no longer able to change a situation, we are challenged to change ourselves. Between stimulus and response there is a space. In that space is our power to choose our response. In our response lies our growth and our freedom."

Let that sink in. As you and your team navigate the stormy seas of change, as a creator of your own destiny, never forget that no matter what happens you get to choose your response. Do not give your power away to other people.

BE A CHALLENGER, NOT A PERSECUTOR

While being a persecutor focussed on blame, anger and finger-pointing is not helpful during a change, that doesn't mean you have to simply go meekly along with what may be poor decisions from above. We need challengers in the workplace. The key is to challenge in an effective and appropriate way.

In the role of challenger (which is what this whole chapter is about), your focus is on fostering improvement, learning and growth. You ask constructive questions in a bid to develop better outcomes. You evoke action and hold others to account in a respectful way.

Examples of challenger questions include: "Does it have to be done this way?" "How could we do it differently?" "Is this the best way to achieve the result we're after?"

The challenger does not only challenge ideas but the responses and behaviour of people as well. But rather than do this in an aggressive way that pulls others down, as the persecutor would, the challenger builds others up. "You can do this," they might say to a wavering member of the team. "You can choose your response here."

BE A COACH NOT A RESCUER

And instead of rescuer, TED* features the role of coach. A lot has been written about the importance of leaders being coaches – and for good reason. A leader who coaches others is compassionate; they support, encourage, empower and assist their people but recognise it is not their job to jump in and fix everything as a rescuer would. They understand that other people need to do the work themselves because saving the day is only an unsustainable short-term fix. People need to want to help themselves.

In the role of coach, a leader will teach other people and delegate, rather than do everything for them. They will ask great questions that help another person find clarity to create their own vision and action plan for navigating their way through change. *"How do you want to get through and emerge from this change?"* You might ask. *"What do you want to be known for?"* *"What could you do differently?"* *"How will you do it?"*

We're going to explore the role of leader as coach in depth as it applies to leading through change in the next chapter as we look at the fourth concept in this Five Cs model – Coach with Compassion.

Once you understand the Drama Triangle and TED* models you start seeing people operating from the positions within them everywhere. And while victims and persecutors can often appear to dominate during tough times, I've also seen people operate from creator mode in the most extreme circumstances, much like Viktor Frankl did.

Tanisha Smitherson, founder of Gippsland Latrobe Aboriginal Advocacy and Support, learned about the two triangles in a workshop with me in 2019. The models stuck with her and Tanisha used them to challenge her own mindset during extreme trauma and life changes. This is her story, shared with her permission.

In December 2020, Tanisha went into hospital for day surgery. What was meant to be a simple procedure ended in her needing a femoral bypass on her right leg. When the stitches were removed, her thigh opened up and in went a hospital superbug. Tanisha developed a devastating infection and after a long year and a half battle, it ended with surgeons having to amputate both of Tanisha's legs.

In March 2022, Tanisha sent me an email. Now a bilateral amputee, Tanisha said initially she couldn't fathom going through life with no legs. But then she began to think.

"In my head I imagined that I was standing on a balcony and looking at the situation from above. Many thoughts ran through my head, some of them very dark. But then, I also remembered the Five Cs from your workshop and the triangles," she wrote to me.

"I realised I needed to stop playing the victim and despite the fact there was a lot in my life that I couldn't control or influence, I could control my headspace and I could choose and control my response to the situation.

"It hasn't been easy. Life is damn hard but I'm getting there. I'm so glad that I attended your session, because without that knowledge and understanding I don't know that I would have made it through."

Every time I read Tanisha's words they make me sit back in my seat, shake my head and wonder how I would handle the challenge and change she has been through. What a remarkable woman. And what an incredible example of the power of challenging your mindset to lead yourself through extreme change.

HOW TO CHALLENGE MINDSETS WITH CANDOUR USING THE DRAMA TRIANGLE AND THE EMPOWERMENT DYNAMIC

So how do you do it? How do you shift from one model of mindset and response under pressure to the other? How do you challenge yourself with candour to show up from The Empowerment Dynamic rather than the Drama Triangle as you and your team navigate change?

Let's start with you.

1. Acknowledge where you're at

The first step to shifting from the Drama Triangle to The Empowerment Dynamic is acknowledging where you're at. This can be confronting. It requires great courage, candid self-reflection, and a willingness to challenge yourself to be vulnerable. But as I've said, you can't change what you don't acknowledge so you have to start here.

2. Choose where you want to be

The next step is to make a choice about where you want to be. It's as simple and as incredibly difficult as that. Don't confuse simple and easy. Shifting out of the Drama Triangle is one of the hardest things you'll ever do. But it's not complicated. Why do so many people live their lives from a position in the Drama Triangle? Because it's easier. You can just blame everyone else for your problems. Choosing to take personal responsibility for your response and create your own reality, regardless of how challenging the change, is hard. And I mean HARD. But it changes everything. Like it did for Tanisha.

3. Make a plan

Create a personal game plan of action you will take to help you operate from The Empowerment Dynamic as much as possible. Build self-reflection into your day.

For me, that means reflecting on which position in the triangles I've showed up from each day while I'm brushing my teeth at night. It was James Clear who wrote in his brilliant book *Atomic Habits* that if you want to create a new habit, the best way to do it is to attach it to an existing habit. So that's what I did. I may have good intentions to reflect on the triangles each day but unless I attached it to another existing habit, I was unlikely to stick with it. So, I printed out the models and stuck them to the wall in my bathroom where I brush my teeth. I never forget to brush my teeth, and so reflecting on the triangles each evening has become part of my daily routine.

An important point to make here: many people won't operate from one position in the triangles. In fact, it's totally normal to shift around positions in both triangles multiple times within any given day. It doesn't make you a bad person if you dip into the Drama Triangle at times. The key is to raise your awareness of when you do this so that you can take action to consciously make the shift back to The Empowerment Dynamic.

Challenging your team

Let me start with what NOT to do. What I'm not suggesting is to say to your team, or one of your staff: "I think you're in victim mode and you need to snap out of it." That will not go down well and is likely to create disconnection and defensiveness. What I am suggesting, is this:

1. Introduce the two triangles

Make some time with your team to talk through the two triangles. If possible, share a story about how they have helped you deal with challenges and change in your own life.

2. Ask them to reflect on where they are at

Encourage your team to think about where they're spending most of their time at the moment.

3. Ask them where they want to be

Ask your team where they want to operate from more often and why this is important to them.

Use some of the questions in Chapter 6, and ask them where they want to be at the end of the change process. What outcome do they want? Is it to retain their jobs? To still enjoy going to work?

Be candid with them about the damage the Drama Triangle can do to them personally and as a team and focus on the outcomes instead.

4. Challenge them to choose

Challenge your team to choose its response in the face of the change and convey the importance of not giving your power away. Create ways of checking in with each other and holding each other accountable.

Reflecting on these models and the words of Viktor Frankl is incredibly powerful but can also be confronting for some. There are people who have been raised with a victim mindset who have lived that way their entire lives. You introducing these concepts may be a significant challenge to the way the person thinks, at a time when they are already under stress. However, it is often exactly what someone spiralling during a change needs. It's like the slap in the face when someone is panicking to help them regain focus, with curiosity and compassion on either side of this challenge.

CHALLENGE UNFETTERED OPTIMISM

While many people fall into the Drama Triangle and spiral into negativity during change, some people go to the other extreme, falling into unfettered optimism, avoidance and toxic positivity.

You know the sort: the people who put their hands over their ears and sing "la, la, la", as if pretending the change isn't happening or that it won't impact them will make it so. Or those who believe that no matter how dire or difficult the situation is, the answer is "just be positive". These people dismiss negative emotions and respond to distress in others with false reassurances of "she'll be right" rather than empathy and understanding.

Both approaches – being overly negative or positive – can be damaging and that's where the Stockdale Paradox comes in. The Stockdale Paradox is the ability to balance optimism with realism to get through tough times when the future is uncertain. It's a concept that is very relevant when leading yourself and others through change.

The Stockdale Paradox was named after James Stockdale, the highest-ranking US military officer held captive in the infamous "Hanoi Hilton" POW camp during the Vietnam War.

He was imprisoned for eight years from 1965 to 1973 and repeatedly tortured.

In 2001, American author and business expert, Jim Collins wrote about Stockdale in his classic business book, *Good to Great*. In a wide-ranging interview, Collins asked Stockdale how he dealt with the trauma and uncertainty of captivity for so many years. After all, he never knew if he was going to survive the day, if he was going to be tortured, or if and when the war was ever going to end.

This is what Stockdale said: "I never lost faith in the end of the story...I never doubted not only that I would get out, but also that I would prevail."

But then he added: "You must never confuse faith that you will prevail in the end – which you can never afford to lose – with the discipline to confront the most brutal facts of your current reality, whatever they might be."

Collins went on to call this approach of being resilient through life's challenges "The Stockdale Paradox".

It's about hoping for the best, while being prepared for and facing up to the worst. You need to embrace both optimism and realism to get through.

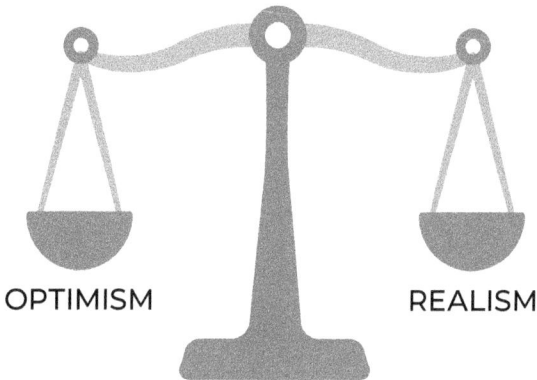

OPTIMISM   REALISM

In my leading through change workshops, I ask leaders to tell me the brutal facts of their current reality when it comes to whatever change it is that they are dealing with at the time. "Don't hold back," I tell them. "Hit me with your challenges as frankly and candidly as you can. Tell me what you're thinking but haven't spoken until now."

After capturing them all on a whiteboard I turn back to the group and say, "Righto, those are the facts of your current reality. They are what they are and we can't shy away from them. Now, what are you going to do about them? It's not about being negative. It's not about getting bogged down in a bitch and whinge fest. It's about being real. Once you face up to the brutal facts of your reality – like the fact that change is hard – you can create a game plan for how to deal with it."

In one workshop with a group of mine and power station workers, their brutal facts included "the board could choose to close us even earlier than the advertised date" and "people are going to jump ship to find new jobs before we close. We're going to haemorrhage good staff". Both very valid and possible concerns. What followed was a fantastic discussion about the importance of good leadership in retaining staff and how critical it was to continue operating and maintaining the plant to a high standard to make it difficult for the board to make a decision to go early. Never had good leadership been more important and it was only through discussing the brutal facts that this realisation landed for many in the room. Did it guarantee good staff would stay and the station wouldn't be shut early? No, of course not. Those things could absolutely happen and the leaders had to be prepared for that. But, by facing up to it they could minimise the chance of it happening and also be prepared for it if it did.

As American motivational writer William Arthur Ward wrote, "The pessimist complains about the wind; the optimist expects it to change; the realist adjusts the sails." What sails can you and your team adjust to get through this change in the best shape possible?

Interestingly, both Stockdale and Viktor Frankl were asked who didn't survive the wars. Their response? The optimists. Because they always thought the war was going to end on Saturday, and then it didn't. So they picked a new date and said "Christmas, it will definitely be done by then", only it wasn't. In the end, hope was lost and they died of broken hearts.

I used the Stockdale Paradox many times during the COVID pandemic to prepare myself for the likelihood of further lockdowns and of my kids going back to remote learning. Like it was for so many, remote learning was HARD yakka in my house. I had three primary school-aged boys who wouldn't do any schoolwork unless I was sitting at the table with them, I was running a full-time business 100% online, and trying to keep the house running too. I so hoped that remote learning was over – I had optimism – BUT, in true Stockdale Paradox mode, I was also realistic and prepared myself for the possibility that the boys may end up learning from home with me again. I thought about how I would make it work if that happened. I looked at the lessons I'd learned up until then and what I would do differently next time. And then, when the last lockdown in late 2021 was announced in Victoria, I was prepared. Rather than react, I was able to respond because I had prepared myself for that eventuality. It wasn't easy, in fact it was still incredibly tough, but I had a game plan ready to go.

When navigating uncertainty and change it can be tempting to shy away from the hard parts, but this is where we need to challenge ourselves and our teams to face up to the brutal facts of our current reality with candour.

1. What are the brutal facts of your current reality as a leader steering your people through the storm of change, and as part of a team navigating it?
2. What's your game plan for facing up to them?

Remember, everyone responds to change differently so the brutal facts may be different for different people within your team and you can talk this through with people individually when you coach with compassion (see Chapter 8).

CHALLENGE BEHAVIOURS

Behaviour is more important to manage than performance. Or rather, behaviour is a core component of performance. Yet far too often leaders let poor behaviour go unchecked because someone is considered a "good operator". Nothing kills culture quicker than poor behaviour, particularly if it is excused and not addressed. It doesn't matter if that person is your star salesperson or machinery operator, if they are allowed to behave poorly, the message that sends to the rest of the team is that the behaviour is acceptable.

It is particularly important to be aware of this at times of stress, pressure, challenge and change. Yes, you absolutely have to be empathetic and understanding that your people are doing it tough, but you also have to hold them and yourself accountable for behaviour.

The best way to do that is to first make your expectations clear. As a team, discuss your shared expectations for performance and behaviour as you navigate the change. Don't leave things unsaid. Don't assume people will "just get on with it". Address the elephant in the room and put it all on the table. This is where you incorporate the first two C concepts with challenge with candour.

You need to be clear, you need to connect and be curious, but you also need to hold people accountable.

You need to make it very clear that despite the pressure, everyone still needs to take personal responsibility for how they show up.

This requires candid conversations. It's not the time to be vague and assume "they should know" what good behaviour looks like. This is when you need to be absolutely clear and direct about what the expectations are, and then hold people to account for upholding them. Ideally, you create these expectations together as a team.

If you don't do this. If you don't set clear and consistent expectations for behaviour and performance, it can get messy very quickly. Tolerance levels become non-existent, niggles become explosions, stress immobilises, some people give up and go missing in action, while others go off on stress leave or create conflict in almost every interaction. Culture, performance, behaviour and team dynamics can fall apart and good people will leave.

So how do you do it? How do you challenge behaviour with candour while leading change? Well, it's a whole lot easier if you've created shared expectations for behaviour as a team before the change has even happened. That way, when the change hits you're just reinforcing and holding people accountable for behaviours that are already clear and understood. If you're not leading through a change right now and you haven't had this conversation with your team already, then I recommend you do it as soon as possible. And if you are in the thick of change and you haven't developed clear behavioural expectations? Never fear, you can still do it now. Here's are a few suggestions for how:

Above and below the line

Get your people together in a room with a whiteboard and ask them to think about the worst people they've ever worked with, particularly at times of pressure. How did those people communicate and behave? Ask them to think about people they've worked with across their entire career, not just at the organisation you're with now, and challenge them to get specific about what the person did that made them not good to work with. Make it clear they are not allowed to name names! Capture all of these negative behaviours on the bottom half of the whiteboard.

Next, ask your people to think about the best people they've ever worked with under pressure. How did those people communicate and behave? What did they do specifically that made them good to work with? Capture these words on the top half of the same whiteboard, then draw a line between the two. That line is called the line of choice.

In my workshops, here's what I say next:

It's really easy to throw all those words up there when you're thinking about other people, but now I want you to turn them back on yourselves. Think about how you communicate and behave under pressure. If you're really honest with yourself. If you put down your excuses and justifications, do you operate above or below the line?

People who operate below the line are not bad people, but they don't make a choice about how they show up. In most cases they just react and go where their emotions take them. They deny, blame, justify and defend, and don't take personal responsibility for their own actions.

People who operate above the line make a conscious decision about how they show up. They choose to take personal responsibility for their communication and behaviour, even when it's hard. They are accountable for what they do.

We all dip below the line sometimes but we need to be more conscious of when we do it and try our best to operate above the line as much as possible.

One of the things I love about this very simple model and activity is that it creates shared language and a way of calling out poor behaviour in a non-confrontational way. It allows you to say things to colleagues like, "Mate, that's a bit below the line. Come on, we want to operate above the line, remember?"

What does good behaviour and performance through change look like?

I often use above and below the line as a springboard into a conversation about what good performance and behaviour through change actually looks like. This is about taking individual words and putting them into sentences with more meat on the bones. If you want people to be kind to each other, what does kind actually look like in practice? Can you describe it? It's hard to hold your people to account for their behaviour if you and they are not clear on what they are being held to account for. Set everyone up for success. The more specific you and your people are about what good behaviour through change looks like, the better.

Yes, it will get stressful. No, people will not always be at their best. But what are the baseline expectations for how you all show up during this tough time? Discuss it, name it and make sure everyone in the room is on the same page in being able to explain it.

What will we do, what won't we do?

After discussing what good behaviour through change looks like in practice, I like to drill down further and help the team get even more specific about the actions and standards they commit to living by. Challenge your people to come up with a handful of specific, plain speak, core behaviours or ground rules that they commit to upholding under pressure. This can then become a team charter that people sign up to.

Frame it by asking your people:

1. What will we always do?
2. What will we never do?

Get each person to come up with one suggestion each – an action or behaviour that they believe will have the biggest impact on how the team shows up and works well together during the change. Don't let them settle for generic statements like "We will treat each other with respect." It's too vague – respect means different things to different people. Drill down. Perhaps it's "we will get curious not furious" by asking questions rather than making assumptions, or "assume positive intent". Maybe you go with "say it sooner" or "address the elephant" and commit to speaking up and having conversations early rather than holding onto feedback and avoiding tough conversations. Even super simple and practical behaviours like "we will say hello to everyone in the morning" or "we will ensure everyone has the chance to speak in meetings by going around the room" can hit the mark if that will address a challenge that causes issues in your team. This is about what works for you and your people and what will have the biggest impact on culture, behaviour and performance.

Once you brainstorm your "always do" and "never do" behaviours, it's time to cut the list back. You don't want a shopping list of 20 behaviours – no one will remember them and then no one will live them. While you may start out there, ideally you want to cut it back to a top three to six behaviours that really speak to your people. Get these behaviours right, and I often find that living them addresses most of the conflict in teams. It's the old 80/20 Pareto Principle: 80 per cent of the problems are addressed by focussing 20 per cent of the possible ground rules.

How do you get your team to cut the list back? My favourite way is to write each behaviour on a giant sticky note, stick it to the wall and then give everyone three to five sticky dots to vote with. Once you've voted and have a top three to six, type them up, print them out, and put them where people will see them. I have seen teams create business cards and postcards with their behaviour charter or team rules printed on them. Some even write up charters that they have people sign off on. Not only does this help people to keep their behaviour in check, but also it makes it easier for you to hold them accountable, and for you to onboard any new people into the team.

What's ok, what's not ok

The reality is, even if you do all of the activities (which I highly recommend you do), some of your people are going to behave poorly at times during uncertainty and change. When that happens, it is up to you as the leader to hold them accountable for this. And the best way I've found to do that is using a simple yet powerful "what's ok, what's not ok" framework for conversations. What I love about this framework (apart from its simplicity) is that it balances care, connection and empathy with challenge and accountability.

Here's a few examples of what it looks like in practice:

- *"It's ok to feel stressed and apprehensive about this change but what's not ok is to yell at me or your colleagues in a meeting."*
- *"I appreciate you're angry and disappointed about the change. That's ok. What's not ok is to roll your eyes, slam the table and storm out of the office."*
- *"It's ok to be upset by this decision and to need time to process it. What's not ok is to refuse to do your tasks and be rude to your colleagues."*

Acknowledge the emotion (remember, there are no bad emotions and people are allowed to feel) while also holding the person accountable for their behaviour.

Organise a meeting with your team to discuss shared expectations for performance and behaviour during the change. You may choose to do one of the activities listed above. You may choose to do them all. The key is to involve your people in the process and ask them about their expectations of you and each other, not just dictate your expectations to them.

CHALLENGE GROUP THINK AND THE SQUEAKY WHEEL

"We all think it's a terrible idea," Kimberly said at the start of the meeting about a new procurement system being introduced in her workplace. "It's just going to make our jobs harder and mean everything takes longer. The way we've always done it works and we don't think this change is necessary."

Kimberly glared around the room as if challenging her colleagues to contradict her. No one did. The group was happy for Kimberly to do the thinking and advocating for them. It was easier to go along with whatever she said.

Managing "group think" is often one of the biggest challenges leaders face as they try to influence the mindset and behaviour of their people during times of change. Group think happens when a group of people agree, come to a consensus, or make decisions collectively without critical reasoning or discussion. It's particularly common in teams that have at least one vocal negative person who carries sway with others, and it results in decisions and opinions being unchallenged while at the same time presented as universally agreed.

In order to challenge group think and manage the person who is the squeaky wheel, you need the tools to facilitate group discussions effectively and "manage the angry mob".

In any group of people, you tend to have a small number of supporters (hopefully at least one). These are the people who like you as a person and know you are well intentioned. At the other end of the spectrum, you have the haters. These are the people who don't like you or the organisation and will disagree with anything you say, simply because it was you who said it. Hopefully your team doesn't have too many people in this camp, but having worked in some rough industries over the years, I know having a high number of haters is the reality for some leaders. And then in the middle, you have the mob. Usually the biggest group, these are the people who are undecided about how they feel and can be swayed either way.

The mistake many leaders make is to spend too much time trying to convince the haters that the change isn't bad and that they should get on board. By focussing so much time on the negative group, all you do is bring the mob over to that side. That is not what you want. The mob is who you need to focus on in this situation. As the saying goes, "haters gonna hate", whether you try to convince them or not. Sure, you need to manage their behaviour (more on that in a sec) but you're probably wasting your breath trying to get them on side. Instead, focus on influencing the mob – they're the ones who can be swayed.

What happens if you don't manage the mob? Mob rule can take over! If they're not influenced by you, this group of people will likely be influenced by the vocal haters and then you're in real trouble.

This concept was core to training I ran with leaders in the construction industry during new enterprise bargaining agreement (EBA) negotiations. Each leader had to present the proposed changes to their team and they were not popular. In fact, there was a serious chance that the presentations could get totally out of hand with yelling, swearing and threatening. Managing the angry mob and challenging group think was essential. Here's some tips for how to do that.

MANAGING THE ANGRY MOB

Step 1. Set ground rules at the start

- Explain how the meeting will run. If you want people to hold their questions until the end of your presentation, you need to ask them to do that right from the get-go.

- Outline the behaviour that's acceptable during the meeting. Boundaries are important. The "what's ok what's not ok" approach is a good one to include here: *"It's ok to be concerned and angry and have questions, but what I ask is that you treat me and others in the room with respect. And what respect looks like to me is please put your hand up if you have a question, let's not yell or swear."*

- Manage dominant voices by using the one question and move on rule. *"To make sure all voices are heard, once you've asked a question or made a comment, we'll move on to anyone else in the room who has a question or comment before we come back to anyone for a second go. Does that work for you?"* You want to get them to a yes. Again, success is in the set-up and it's crucial you outline your expectations at the start of the meeting. If not, when you try to move on from the dominant voice, it will look like you're trying to avoid their questions.

Step 2. Explain the scope

▸ Be clear on what's in and what's out of the conversation. What's on the table for discussion and what's not? This was something I had to articulate explicitly during a workshop I facilitated between government agencies, emergency service organisations and user groups on trail bike safety in Gippsland. There are a lot of issues and concerns about trail bike safety in general, but we were not there to get bogged down and distracted by them. We were there to talk specifically about trail bike safety in Gippsland and my role as facilitator was to keep them to that.

▸ Outline what you'll do if you can't answer a question or the question does not fit in the scope. Will you take the question on notice? If you do, be clear about how and when you'll follow up with the answer. Will you use a "parking lot" to capture questions and concerns that don't fit in the scope? If so, what will happen with it after the meeting? Be clear.

Step 3. Help them drill down to identify specific concerns

I once sat in on a presentation about an upcoming change in which a participant responded to the news by saying, "The whole thing is shit." Although it might be a person's initial reaction, "the whole thing is shit" is not a response you can do anything with – and you need to tell your people that. You need to help them drill down to what their specific concern is, and explain the reason why this is important. You may try:

"I hear that you're not happy with the change and I want to listen to your concerns and take them to management, but I can't do anything with 'the whole thing is shit'. What is it specifically about the change that you don't like?" Keep asking what and why questions until the person is able to articulate their concerns. Be patient, this may take a while but it has a number of benefits.

Firstly, it quickly helps you identify if the person has genuine concerns or if they're just lobbing bombs and resisting for the fun of it. Secondly, it helps you uncover more specifically what the concerns are and puts you in a better position to then be able to address them.

This happened to a leader I worked with in the mining industry. The leader was charged with rolling out a new camera system across the site for monitoring faults and one of his staff was vehemently against it. He was oppositional, resistant and defiant. The new camera system was not going to work and he was going to have no part in it, he told his boss. Rather than react with a command and control, aggressive "Are you refusing a work order?" question, the leader called the staff member in for a one-on-one conversation. He then asked the staff member to help him understand why he believed the camera system was a bad idea. By being curious and continuing to challenge with probing questions, the leader helped the staff member narrow in from "it's stupid and it's never going to work" to "our cameras don't have the capability to do that and if we want a system like that we'd have to invest in a different camera set-up". This is where the leader got really smart. Capitalising on the staff member's obvious passion and interest, he tasked the man with researching what he believed the best camera set-up would be to make the new system and software work. The man took on the role with gusto and came back to the leader a week later with his suggestion. The leader was then able to take this up the chain to management, highlighting both the initial problem and the solution the staff member had come up with. Management agreed with the recommendation and the leader was then able to take this news back to his staff member. The man who started out as the resistant detractor ended up being the system's biggest champion.

Step 4. Use levels of consensus to identify where people are at and make group decisions when required

Gaining consensus in group decision-making can be hard, particularly if you're asking for a yes/no answer.

When people are only given the options of supporting or opposing a change, it can be tricky to get even simple decisions over the line, or to know how strong the approval (if you get it) really is.

Those with questions may vote no simply because they need more information.

And those who vote yes may do so begrudgingly despite their reservations, creating issues when you need to deliver on the decision down the track.

So how can you do things differently? How can you break through group think and gain consensus on a decision in a timely way but with more nuance and understanding of where people really sit?

One of my favourite tools to use in these situations is Levels of Consensus.

Rather than asking for a yes/no response on complex or significant decisions, I ask people to give me a number between one and five.

Here's what those numbers represent:

1. I like it, am on board and can easily accept this decision.
2. I accept this decision but may have some questions/points to clarify at a later time.
3. I can live with this decision even though it may not be my preferred option.
4. I don't agree but I will not block this decision.
5. I loathe it and cannot accept this decision.

I introduce these levels at the start of a meeting and have them projected on a slide, written on a flip chart, or stuck to a giant sticky note on the wall where everyone can see.

I also discuss what number we want/need people to be at for a decision to pass so everyone is clear on how the levels will work.

It may be that we want the majority of people to be at a two and above. Perhaps we agree to have further discussion if there are multiple people at numbers three or four. If we have someone at number five, we might have to negotiate until we can get them to a four or above.

The rules placed around the levels will differ depending on the group or the type of decision being made.

Sometimes I scrap numbers two and five all together and make it a simple: Like it, can live with it, loathe it response.

Even with just three options, you get more information than if you'd only asked for a yes or no.

This can save time, stop you getting bogged down, cut through repetitive debate about the change, and help your group make decisions much more successfully.

Step 5. Know when and how to shut it down

While the first four steps will give you the best chance of a meeting or briefing about change not getting out of hand, they don't guarantee it. That's why knowing when and how to shut a meeting down is important. If your personal safety or that of someone else in the room is threatened, the conversation is harming your cause, ground rules are being ignored, or behaviour has descended into chaos, it's time to call it quits. This is where the concepts of "escalate with notice" and following through come into play.

Re-state your ground rules, why having the conversation is important, your intention and the scope of the meeting. Then, state that if the poor behaviour or disrespectful communication continues, you will have to ask the person or people involved to leave (if it's only a couple of haters) or otherwise end the meeting. Put the ball in their court. If they don't adjust their behaviour, do what you said – shut down the meeting and physically leave.

REFLECTION

Consider the dynamics in your team and whether group think or dominant voices are likely to be an issue as you lead through change. Read back over the strategies outlined in this chapter and decide which ones you'll use with your team. What ground rules can you set at the start of meetings? What facilitation techniques can you use? How can you challenge your people's focus, mindsets and behaviour as they navigate change to ensure they can continue to do good work and behave in an appropriate way?

SUMMARY

In this chapter you've learned how to challenge your own and other people's focus, mindset, unfettered optimism, behaviour and group think. You've also learned about the importance of setting clear expectations with your team. Doing this will not only help you and your team to be more resilient during times of change, it will also help you when faced with any challenge in your life – professionally or personally.

An important reminder here: you need to model the behaviour, mindset and focus you want to see in your people. If you don't do that, your challenge will be for nothing and your candour will be met with distrust, resentment and outright objection.

As I mentioned at the start of this chapter, challenging with candour only works if you've first connected with curiosity. Warmth first, strength second. But it doesn't end here. Now that you've been hard on the issue, it's time to follow up by being soft on the person. Yes, hold them accountable, but support them to get through the change well by coaching them with compassion.

Chapter 8

COACH WITH COMPASSION

The Five Cs

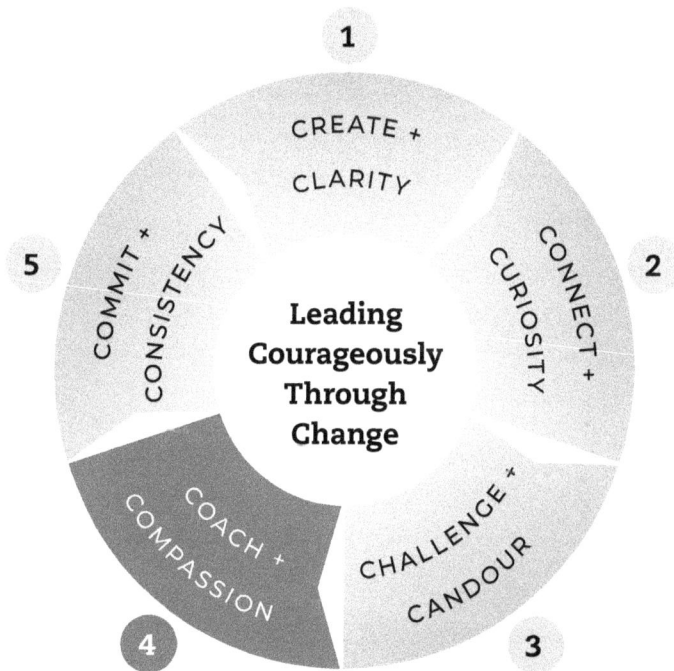

Coach: "Someone whose job is to provide training for people or to help prepare them for something…"
– *Cambridge Dictionary*

Compassion: "The feeling or emotion, when a person is moved by the suffering or distress of another, and by the desire to relieve it."
– *Oxford English Dictionary*

Alicia seemed to take news that she would be out of a job in a few months well. When the initial announcement was made that the program she was part of hadn't been successful in securing government funding for the next financial year, she was pragmatic. When her leader, Pete, ran a briefing with the team she asked a handful of questions calmly while some of her colleagues got angry and upset. For Alicia the news wasn't a total surprise. She knew the funding wasn't a given and that the government was changing its focus. She knew her contract was dependent on the funding being recurring and that losing it meant she would lose her job. She knew it and it looked like she was handling it well.

Because Alicia seemed to be coping and wasn't causing disruption like some of the others, Pete left her alone. "At least I've got one I don't have to worry about," Pete thought. Because Alicia was ok. Until she wasn't.

Unlike her colleagues, Alicia held it together through the initial weeks of the change announcement. It was a couple of months later as the end date loomed that the wheels started to fall off.

Pete didn't notice Alicia was struggling until he finally sat across from her in their scheduled one-on-one catch up. Pete was one of my coaching clients at the time and I'd encouraged him to start holding regular check-ins with each member of his team: not to discuss work and tasks, but to check in with each of his people to see how they were travelling. To connect human to human, get an understanding of where they were at and offer any support that he could.

Alicia was the last member of the team to have her one-on-one with Pete. He'd deliberately left her until last because he thought she was ok. As the saying goes, the squeaky wheel gets the oil, and Alicia was not a squeaky wheel.

Pete was trying a new strategy with his 1:1s and started off by putting the feelings wheel from Chapter 3 in front of Alicia and asking her to pick the two words that best represented where she was at. Alicia looked at the wheel and decided to be honest: "Devastated and terrified," she finally responded, keeping her eyes downcast at the paper. Pete sat up straighter. That was not the answer he had been expecting. But Pete had never asked the question before and so Alicia had not disclosed it.

Once you've provided clarity to your people by giving them clear messaging about the change, you've shown empathy to your team and connected with curiosity, and you've challenged with candour, it's time to work one-on-one with your people to coach them through the change with compassion.

It's important to make a quick distinction here about the difference between mentoring and coaching. A mentor is someone who shares their knowledge, skills, insights and experience to help another person develop and grow. A coach helps that person choose their own direction by asking questions and prompting self-reflection.

In the role of coach and leader through change, you need to support and encourage your people to find their own answers to the challenges they face. It's not about rescuing, problem-solving, providing quick-fix answers, or saving the day. It's also not about pity. It's about asking questions, prompting reflection, and using future-focussed inquiry to help them steer themselves through the storm. Your aim is to support your team members' own insight and to help them take personal responsibility for their actions and mindset. You're supporting them to challenge themselves.

Coaching – like clarifying, connecting and challenging – should be a key part of your leadership toolkit. This is the chance for you as a leader to have a lasting impact on your people.

A lot of what applied in Chapter 6: Connect with Curiosity applies again here, but rather than connecting with your team as a group, we're now focussed on one-on-one. And while empathy is still a key component, in this chapter we're talking about compassion.

Compassion and empathy are what I'd describe as "same, same, but different', to borrow a saying popular in Africa when I travelled there many years ago. They are similar but there is nuanced difference between the two.

While empathy refers more generally to the ability to take the perspective of and connect with the emotions of another person, compassion takes those feelings and thoughts a step further and includes the desire to help the other person. Compassion includes action.

Now, you might be thinking, "But Leah, I have enough on my plate leading through this change as it is. I don't have time for more connection, let alone formal one-on-one meetings."

That's ok, they don't have to be formal one-on-ones (although if you can schedule these on a semi-regular basis I highly recommend it). You can have coaching conversations informally at any time. The key is to make time to have them on a regular basis, and not just with those who you think are struggling. See this as an investment. Rather than think "I don't have time to meet", reframe it to "I don't have time NOT to meet with my people". Influence is all about relationships. If you want to be a more influential leader as you navigate change, you need to build and maintain your relationships.

Taking the time to proactively check in with someone for 30 minutes every few weeks is a lot more efficient than dealing with people problems, low morale, lost productivity and poor behaviour.

It will build trust and give you the chance to really get a feel for who is coping and who isn't. This can allow you to intervene and provide support before things fall apart. It also allows you to discover what your people really think about the change when not in front of their peers. Understanding their fears, uncertainties, insecurities, challenges and career aspirations will increase your ability to lead and influence them.

Many leaders that I've supported to have compassionate coaching conversations with their staff over the years have been surprised by what has been revealed in the discussions. When one staff member disclosed that they were unsatisfied with their role because they weren't given opportunities to step up, the leader responded with "I never knew" to which the staff member responded "Well, you never asked". With good questions, time to listen and a safe space, you may uncover information you would have never otherwise known.

It's also an opportunity to have hard conversations about the future. Some people may need to leave the organisation, upskill or find new jobs as the result of a change. And that's not necessarily a bad thing. Coaching conversations, when held with compassion, can help people reach this realisation, which can be the best outcome for them, the organisation and you.

When Sam asked a long-term member of his team if they were up to learning the new CRM (customer relationship management) system that would fundamentally change the way they did their job, it turns out they weren't.

After some more discussion it was clear to Sam and the staff member that the best way forward was for them to apply for one of the voluntary redundancy packages on offer, rather than hold on and become resentful.

"I'm so grateful that I took the time to have one-on-one conversations with my team about the change," Sam told me. "By uncovering where each person was at, I was able to work with them to identify what support they needed from me and what the best next step was for them. For some people that meant jumping in and learning the new system, for others it meant extra training to help them feel competent in switching from a manual to a cloud-based system, and for others it was helping them realise their role was about to change so fundamentally that this wasn't the job for them anymore. And that was ok."

In her book *The Places That Scare You*, American Buddhist nun Pema Chödrön wrote: "Compassion is not a relationship between the healer and the wounded. It's a relationship between equals [...] Compassion becomes real when we recognise our shared humanity."

This is where I remind you that compassion is not just something you give to other people. You need to recognise your own humanity and give compassion to yourself too.

Yes, you are a leader and your job is to support people through change the best way possible. But you are also human. You are one person. And you need to be kind to yourself. You will make mistakes. You won't always be at your best. You will need to rest. And that's ok. You have to look after yourself through the pressure of change if you want to have any chance of being able to support your people.

That last paragraph was easy to write and is so much harder to do. If I'm really honest with you here, I very much struggle with this myself. Compassion for other people – tick! Compassion for myself – a big red cross. I hold myself to ridiculous standards at times and it doesn't just hurt me, it also hurts my team. If I'm not kind to myself, if I don't take my foot off the accelerator at times, I'm not at my best to lead my people. So rather than seeing self-compassion as a luxury, I want you to see it as a necessity. And if you're still finding it hard, ask yourself, what would I say to a member of my team right now? Make sure you take your own advice too.

Most leaders understand theoretically that coaching and compassion are important parts of their role but many are unclear about how to do it in practice, particularly when they're time poor, have a traditionally managerial style, or are under the extreme pressure of leading change. In this chapter I'll give you some of the basic skills and strategies to help you coach your people with compassion so that they are able to find their own answers to their problems.

THE MOST COMPASSIONATE PEOPLE HAVE BOUNDARIES

Leading through change is often a long game. It takes stamina and resilience. That is why setting, holding and protecting your own personal boundaries is essential. The only way you'll be able to give and maintain compassion to your team through the stress of change is if you're in good shape yourself. And the only way you'll be in good shape is if you protect your own energy and time.

Some leaders think compassion means giving all of themselves to their people. Being there for others at every moment. Saying yes to every request for a conversation. Give, give, give until there's nothing left to give. If this is your view of what compassion looks like, it's no wonder you might be sceptical, thinking, "No Leah, I can't give any more. I'm running on empty already. I can't do compassion too."

Oh, but you can. And boundaries will help you do it. Let me be clear: compassion is NOT about giving until you're empty. That is not a sustainable practice at all. Boundaries – such as setting times for when you're available and not responding to phone calls or emails (unless it's an emergency) after a certain time at night – are not in opposition to compassion. Rather, they are essential for it. Setting and holding boundaries in this way will help you create the space to be ok in the middle of the storm. And that is essential to being able to lead with compassion at a time when you will likely be tested professionally and personally like never before.

This is where the "what's ok, what's not ok" framework is useful again. It's a great way of setting boundaries for yourself with compassion. Here are some examples:

> ▶ *"It's ok for you to vent to me about the change when you need to but what's not ok is to make that venting a personal attack on other people."*

- *"I am happy to discuss the change with you and want to hear how it's affecting you, but now is not a good time for me. Let's see if we can book in a time to catch up this afternoon."*

- *"I know you want to have a confidential conversation with me about this and I'm absolutely here for that, but I don't take work calls after-hours because it's crucial that I give myself time to switch off and reset."*

REFLECTION

Think about the boundaries you could set with your team. Of course, there will always be exceptions when you need to be available to deal with someone who is distressed or in crisis, but what are some of the general boundaries you could create for yourself – at work and at home – to help you show up well?

Here are some examples:

- If you need more than five minutes with me, please book a meeting.

- I don't respond to phone calls or emails after 6pm. If it's an emergency, please send me a text message.

- Please don't interrupt me if my door is closed. That indicates that I'm doing focussed work or in a confidential conversation.

- No meetings before 10am.

- I am happy to hear your concerns about the change but I will shut down any personal attacks against those delivering it.

- Discussing the change and asking questions at the pre-start is encouraged but I will move us on if I feel like the conversation has become unproductive.

Write yourself a list of boundaries and share any that are relevant with your team. Explain the "why" to them when you do it. Make sure they understand this is about you being the best leader you can for them during these tumultuous times. Afterall, you can't pour from an empty cup.

THE STRAW THAT BREAKS THE CAMEL'S BACK – CHANGE FATIGUE IS REAL

Callum was not ok. After being strong and resilient for three years in his role as team leader at a government agency through bushfires that devastated his region, two years of COVID lockdowns and restrictions, and multiple floods, he was done. Cooked. Burned out. Cactus. When his manager announced the introduction of a new procurement system that would change the way Callum's team engaged with contractors, Callum walked out of the office and drove home. At 10am on a Tuesday.

It wasn't that the new procurement system itself that was the issue. Callum knew it was coming and the series of disasters had only delayed its introduction. Rather, it was one change on top of three years of constant and unprecedented change and emergency that tipped Callum over the edge. It was the change that broke the camel's back.

Change fatigue is real. Sometimes it's not the change itself that is the issue – it might even be a positive change that in normal times would be welcomed – rather, it's the fact that it's another change at all that is the problem.

Sometimes people start off being ok with a change but that response itself changes as time goes on. Like it did for Alicia mentioned at the start of this chapter. That's why checking in with your people regularly and showing genuine care about their wellbeing is so important. It's not just your role to deliver the message of change as the leader, or to ask questions, or to challenge. Part of your role is to provide genuine support the whole way through. Asking someone if they're ok shortly after a change is announced is not enough.

Of course, it's not all on you to pick up if someone is not ok, particularly if they are going to great lengths to hide it from you as their leader. But creating an environment where someone feels like they can disclose how they are feeling is important. If you coach your people regularly with compassion you can identify those who are struggling much quicker and help them find a way forward or to engage with the support they need.

> **REFLECTION**
>
> Consider the people in your team. Have you noticed anyone's attitude, behaviour or communication become more negative, antagonistic or despondent over time? How about your own?
>
> If this self-reflection makes you realise you haven't checked in with yourself or a team member for a while, I want you to prioritise making time for this in the next few days.

MAKE TIME TO MEET

The most valuable gift you can give another person is your time, and this is where that gift comes in. Not just at the start of a change process, but repeatedly all the way through.

Make the time to meet regularly one-on-one with your staff. Not to discuss tasks but to check in with them as a person and coach them to their own solutions and decisions.

Now, I appreciate that for some of you, this will a foreign concept. Aside from the once-a-year mandatory performance review meeting, you may never sit down with your people individually to talk about their aspirations, goals, challenges and concerns. If that is you, don't be surprised if your people are suspicious and guarded when you introduce these sessions, particularly at the first few meetings. These are high trust conversations, so if they're new to you I encourage you to consider explaining the purpose of them to your team. Use your words and explain the why. For example:

"Part of my role as a leader is to make sure I'm checking in with you all regularly one-on-one to discuss how you're travelling, particularly during times of change like this. That's not something I've been great at in the past because I've let managing tasks get in the way of leading people. So, I'm going to start scheduling in a 30-minute catch-up once a month so we have the chance to have conversations that matter. It's also an opportunity for you to share with me any concerns you have or ways I can help support you in your role. And it's an opportunity to talk through my expectations too."

The more you normalise the meetings, the more receptive and involved your people will eventually become. But remember, this may take time.

When I talk with leaders about the importance of making the time to meet one-on-one we discuss what cadence might work best for them and their team. There is no right or wrong answer to this – the key is to find something that works for you. And that may take some trial and error.

Here are some ways I've seen leaders build one-on-one coaching conversations into their leadership:

- ▶ Formal one-on-one conversations scheduled into people's calendars once a month (the leader blocks out one full day and knocks them over in that time).

- Leaders scheduling two formal coaching conversations a week into their calendar and rotating staff through so that each staff member has a one-on-one meeting every four to six weeks.

- Informal opportunistic one-on-ones while "walking the floor", saying hi and having a chat (setting a target of one walk-through a week).

- Working alongside staff members and using the opportunity to have one-on-one conversations.

Find a rhythm that works for you and commit to it. Set aside 30 to 45 minutes per conversation and treat these conversations as important as any KPI or deadline you may be working to. Don't let them drop off or get pushed aside, or fall into the trap of discussing task-focussed day-to-day work. It takes discipline not to default into talking about your (or their) to-do list. Yes, that may be the space you feel most comfortable – focussing on tasks. But that is not what these coaching with compassion conversations are about. This is a different type of conversation. This is a human-focussed conversation.

ACTION

Look at your calendar and consider the people in your team. When and where can you schedule one-on-one conversations with them over the next week or month? What cadence or approach would work best for you? Create a one-on-one meeting plan. Whether that's formal, scheduled and structured coaching conversations (read on for some sample questions you may consider including) or setting yourself a target of one or two informal conversations a week. It doesn't matter what it is, but I want you to write it down. And then I want you to stick to it, or at the very least try it out for a month. Don't treat this as an added extra on your to-do list. Treat it as an essential priority you have to make fit.

DIFFERENT STROKES FOR DIFFERENT FOLKS

It's important to acknowledge here that as leaders, each of you reading this book will be in a different position, and all of your people will have different responses and needs when it comes to the support they require during change too. There is no one "right" way to show you care for your people and coach with compassion. It will look different for all of you.

For some – those with direct reports or a staff of say 10 or less – making the time to meet for regular or semi-regular scheduled one-on-one conversations with your people, particularly during times of change, should be achievable and will most definitely be valuable. For others who have a large team, regular one-on-ones may not be possible, so you'll need to find other ways to support your people.

When Andy led a workforce of 170, regular one-on-ones with all his staff were never going to happen. And that's ok. That didn't mean he couldn't have coaching conversations or show compassion and care for his people. It just looked different to what it did when he had three employees early on in his business.

"This is something I've had to wrestle with – trying to get the balance right between caring for your people and not burning out. When I had five employees I knew if one of my installers had an ingrown toenail. I knew everything about my team and that was really powerful because I understood them on a deeply personal level.

"When I got to 20 staff, I still had a good understanding of what was happening in their lives, but I didn't have as much connection with each person because I was so busy with work.

"And when I had 170 staff, it was just not possible to have that same level of connection with them all. That said, to be a good CEO I still needed to care about them, take interest and have an awareness of what was going on in their lives – some understanding of who was struggling and who needed a bit of extra attention.

"It was more about me showing I cared by connecting them in with the support functions we had in the business, like our Employee Assistance Program and our People and Culture team. It might have been a text message to let them know I'm thinking about them rather than a structured one-on-one meeting, or a brief talk while walking the floor rather than an hour-long discussion over coffee. I couldn't do it all and sometimes it was a struggle to get the balance right, but it was still important that even as CEO I coached my people – particularly my direct reports – with compassion."

It's not just whether you have one-on-one conversations or not, the way you approach a coaching conversation will also depend on the person you are dealing with. As we discussed in Chapter 5, knowing your audience and speaking to their motivations and drivers is key.

Ryan, a shift supervisor, had two operators in his team who were nearing retirement. Despite them both having 18 months to go before their end dates, the two men were already in what was jokingly referred to as the "departure lounge". They'd checked out. They were doing the bare minimum and they weren't interested in learning new things because "We're out the door in 18 months anyway".

Ryan knew he had to do something to try to keep the men engaged through until the end. Having two members of his team coast for the next 18 months had the potential to impact productivity within the crew, not to mention put pressure on the other younger operators and cause resentment. So, rather than join the chorus of behind-the-back grumbles about the pair's work ethic, or address it in a forceful performance-management way, Ryan held coaching conversations with each man to address the elephant in the room. Instead of skating around the issue, Ryan acknowledged the challenge of staying engaged when you know retirement is on the horizon.

He then asked each man (both of whom had worked there for more than 30 years and were very proud of their connection to the industry) what sort of legacy they wanted to leave. Ryan tapped into the men's motivations and drivers. Although both had blustered about just being there to collect a pay check, they genuinely did care about the shape they left the crew in. This led to Ryan encouraging the operators to use the last 18 months of their employment to share as much of their valuable knowledge and experience with the other members of the crew as possible. He spoke about them passing on a legacy that they and their older colleagues could be proud of after so many years of work. Not only did this help re-engage the men and give them purpose in their final months, it also ensured a vital knowledge transfer to younger operators, so those 60 years of experience didn't just leave the building in their heads.

THE DOs AND DON'Ts OF GOOD COACHING CONVERSATIONS

How you approach and frame coaching conversations is crucial. As outlined in Chapter 6, the key is to ask questions that are open-ended but that provide direction. This takes practice. As does listening. Really listening. If you're like me, listening to understand, not to respond will take conscious effort. If you're a talker, used to holding and directing the conversation, you may be tempted to fill the silence of your staff member. I want you to fight against that.

Ask a thoughtful question and then embrace the pause. You'll likely be surprised by how often the other person fills it and shares something they wouldn't have otherwise if you give them the space to do so.

There are some basic dos and don'ts you'll want to adhere to in these conversations. If you have coaching conversations regularly already, these won't come as a surprise. Some have even been mentioned already in this book but a reminder won't hurt. And if you are new to this, I encourage you to take note:

DO

- Make enough time to meet. Set aside at least 30 minutes.
- Focus on the person not the task.
- Tailor your approach to suit each individual. Consider their communication style, motivations and circumstance.
- Open with warmth and a genuine "why" for having the coaching conversation. This is particularly important if coaching conversations are new for you. For example:

"Part of my role as a leader is to help you navigate this uncertainty in the best way possible, so I wanted to ask you some questions that I hope will help us both get a clearer picture of where you're at and what you need…" Or, *"I'm meeting with everyone in the team individually to get a good understanding of how the change is impacting you and what I can do as a leader to best support you at this challenging time…"*

- Let them know that what you discuss is confidential. The only exceptions being if they tell you they plan to harm themselves or someone else, or commit a crime (this often gets a laugh from my coaching clients). You might tell them you're going to share the general "vibe" from the team with upper management after you have spoken with everyone, but make it clear that's as far as you'll go, unless they share something they want you to pass on to others.

- Ask open, person-focussed questions and listen, really listen.

- Make an observation. *"I've noticed…What's up?"*

- Go where the conversation needs to go. This may mean moving away from some of the questions you had planned to ask. Be prepared to adapt and respond to the person's needs.

- Acknowledge, don't dismiss feelings.

- Seek to understand, support and empathise, not to problem-solve or fix.

- Clarify and repeat back to ensure you're clear. *"What I'm hearing is…"*

- Be vulnerable and share something of yourself to encourage the other person to share and show that it's a safe space.

- Embrace the pause.

- Respect if someone doesn't want to share. It may take a few conversations for them to feel comfortable opening up.

- Ask what you can do to help them. Remember, while not about rescuing, compassion differs from empathy in that you are trying to help.

- If you're providing feedback to someone on their behaviour in response to the change, try to feed forward rather than back. Ask future-focussed questions that look for the learnings, such as:

"How else could you look at it?"

"What could you do differently next time?"

"What did you learn and how could you respond in a more appropriate way in the future?"

- Ask for permission if you want to take notes and explain what they'll be used for (perhaps for you to keep track of any actions so you can follow up next time). Taking notes without permission is a sure-fire way to get someone to shut down.

- If you say you're going to follow up, make sure you do! Accountability for yourself and them is important.

DON'T

- Get weird. What do I mean by this? Don't launch into heavy and uncomfortable questions with no warm up or explanation about what you're doing. How you show up is important. If you're obviously awkward, it will make the other person awkward.

- Go outside your wheelhouse – you're not a psychologist or counsellor. Yes, offer support, empathy and compassion but don't get caught offering advice that you're not qualified to give. That is not your role. For more on what to do if someone is not ok, read on.

- Fill every gap in conversation.

- Try to problem solve or rescue them from all their concerns and issues.

- Disagree with how they say they feel or what they describe their experience of the change to be. Their experience is their experience.

- Move on because emotions are uncomfortable.

- Hold so close to your question list that the conversation feels like a "tick and flick" exercise rather than a genuine conversation with care and compassion.

- Fall into the trap of one-upmanship. "Well, if you think you've got it bad, you should hear how hard Kathy is doing it!"

- Make assumptions.

- Say "I know how you feel". You don't.

- Push someone to open up if they've made it clear they don't want to. Just like you've asked your people to respect your boundaries, you have to respect theirs.

- Get sucked into "bitch fests" or rants. Remember your role as the leader.

- Lose your cool or threaten. Stay calm. Breathe. And make it clear what is and isn't ok.

ONE-ON-ONE QUESTION OPTIONS

So now that you understand why coaching with compassion is important and how to go about it, here is a list of questions you may consider asking your staff members in your one-on-one sessions. You don't have to ask all or any of them. Rather, use them as a guide and prompt. Pick out those that work for you, try some out, and discard those that don't fit:

- How are you travelling, really?

- If you had to use two words to describe how you're feeling today (or about the change in general), what would they be? (Use the feelings wheel from Chapter 3 to help draw out if they're frustrated, overwhelmed, angry, stressed, etc.).

- What does successfully navigating this change look like for you?

- ▸ What do you want to be known for as we go through this change?
- ▸ Tell me more about...
- ▸ What has gone well? What has been your biggest win?
- ▸ What has been your biggest learning?
- ▸ What have you noticed in yourself or others?
- ▸ What are you finding most challenging?
- ▸ What would you do differently next time?
- ▸ What do you need to keep, stop or start doing personally to be ok as we navigate this change?
- ▸ What is something that you're doing that is self-sabotaging your success and wellbeing?
- ▸ If you had a magic wand, what change would you make to improve the performance of our team?
- ▸ If you were the decision-maker, how would you implement the change?
- ▸ What do you need from me/how can I help?
- ▸ What's your focus for the next few weeks?
- ▸ Where do you want to be and how do you want to feel in six months when this change is implemented?

Remember, this is not an exhaustive list. I encourage you to use it as a base from which to develop your own coaching questions.

DON'T BE TEMPTED TO PROBLEM-SOLVE, SOMETIMES PEOPLE JUST WANT YOU TO LISTEN

One of the points I've touched on in this chapter and earlier in the book is that empathy does not equal problem-solving. I want to expand on that a bit here because this is a well-intentioned mistake that many leaders make when someone on their team comes to them with a problem, a concern or to express their feelings. Rather than listen, the leader jumps straight into problem-solver mode. They try to fix it, want to rescue the person, or maybe they want to offer advice because they're under pressure and it's quicker. Oftentimes it's because the leader genuinely wants to help them. They want to make it better. But a lot of the time this is not what that other person is actually after and it's not what they need. Sometimes we express our feelings to simply be seen and heard, not because we want someone to fix it but because we simply want someone to listen. We want someone to bear witness to our experience.

So how can you get better at doing this as a leader? How can you get better at coaching rather than problem-solving in your conversations with staff? The answer is simple: ask them what they want and need from you. Instead of jumping straight in with advice when someone shares a concern about the change or a problem with you, try something like this instead:

"Wow, that sounds really challenging. How can I best support you here? Would you like me to offer advice? Share my experience of a similar situation? Give you some possible solutions? Or do you just want me to listen?"

You may be surprised by how often someone responds by saying, "You know what? I just need to vent and for someone to listen. Thanks for doing that for me."

The other benefit of standing back and asking people what they need from you is that it encourages them to find their own ideas and solutions, and that is what coaching is all about.

WHAT TO DO WHEN THEY'RE NOT OK

Coaching conversations are powerful. Sometimes showing you care and creating space for someone to share can expose challenges you didn't know existed. You may discover someone on your team is not coping with the change at all. Knowing what to do if this happens can save a life.

"But Leah, this is exactly why I avoid getting personal with my people! I don't want to ask how they're travelling because I'm totally out of my depth if they say they are struggling. I'd prefer to keep the conversation to work and their tasks and leave the personal stuff to the professionals." I have heard a version of this response from many leaders over the years and I've talked them through it. Because here's the reality: you have a responsibility to care for your people as their leader, particularly when they are navigating difficult change at work. You don't have to be a counsellor or psychologist, you don't have to be a mental health expert, but you do need to care, and with some basic strategies for how to respond you will be able to support your people to get the help they need from the right professionals.

Still not convinced? Let me put it this way, if someone had a heart attack in front of you at work, would you just walk away without doing anything because you're not a doctor? Would that be an acceptable response? No, of course not. The same goes for if one of your staff is suffering emotionally or mentally. You don't walk away. You provide first aid. And that's what this is about – providing FIRST aid. Not all the aid. Just the initial emergency response.

I am a huge advocate of mental health first aid training and encourage leaders to do it in some form with a reputable provider. Having the skills to respond effectively when someone is not ok is essential.

Remember, you don't have to "fix" them or solve all the problems for them. You just need to be there.

As organisational psychologist and bestselling author Adam Grant wrote on social media: "In hard times, people don't want to be told to look on the bright side. They want to know you're on their side. Even if you can't help them feel better, you can always help them feel seen. The best way to support others is not to cheer them up. It's to show up."

So how can you respond if a member of your team discloses that they are not ok? Below is a summary of the ALGEE mental health first aid action plan taught by Mental Health First Aid Australia. As you can see, it's simple and doesn't require you to be anything more than human:

Approach the person, assess and assist with any crisis

Listen and communicate non-judgementally

Give support and information

Encourage the person to get appropriate professional help

Encourage other supports

Here are some further suggestions:

- Educate yourself on the resources and agencies available to support someone who is struggling. This may include your company's Employee Assistance Program (EAP); local general practitioners, psychologists and mental health services; and national organisations such as Beyond Blue, Lifeline, Mindfull Aus and more.

- Have the details of these agencies on hand before you start a coaching conversation so you can provide the information to a staff member during the meeting if required.

- Open in a non-confrontational way using questions or statements outlined earlier in this chapter, such as:

  "I've noticed...What's up?"

  "How are you travelling, really?"

"This is a really challenging time and it's really normal for it to be having an impact on us. I wanted to check in, are you ok?"

- Encourage them to seek assistance and normalise it for them. Be vulnerable yourself and consider sharing if you've used these services before.
- Offer to help them make an appointment if they're open to it.
- Make sure you understand your organisation's policy in regard to stress or mental health leave and provide this information if appropriate.
- Schedule time to follow up with the person and stick to it.
- Make sure you informally check in and follow up too.

If the person is in crisis and discloses that they really are not ok and you are concerned they may be considering harming themselves, do not leave them alone. Call a mental health triage service for advice and link them in with professional help.

I'm very aware this is a heavy topic but it's important to address it in this book, even if briefly. If you haven't done mental health first aid training I highly recommend you put it up near the top of your to-do list. There are short three-hour sessions and longer two-day intensive programs available through a range of providers Australia wide.

In addition, here are some other helpful resources:

- Suicide Call Back Service: 1300 659 467 (telephone counselling for people who are suicidal, available 24 hours a day, 7 days a week)
- Lifeline: 13 11 14 (24 hour-a-day crisis support and suicide prevention)

Mental health crisis numbers:

- ACT: Mental health triage service 1800 629 354
- NSW: Access Mental Health Line 1800 011 511

- NT: Northern Territory mental health services 1800 682 288
- QLD: 1300 MH CALL triage service 1300 642 255
- SA: Mental Health Triage Service 13 14 65
- TAS: Access Mental Health 1800 332 388
- VIC: SuicideLine Victoria 1300 651 251
- WA: Mental Health Emergency Response Line 1800 676 822
- Beyond Blue: beyondblue.com.au

ACTION

1. Book into a mental health first aid course.
2. Gather the contact details of key people and services who can support your staff, including:
   - EAP (Employee Assistance Program).
   - Career counsellor.
   - Medical clinic.
   - Suicide prevention and mental health service providers.

SUMMARY

In this chapter we've further explored the power of showing you care, asking questions, and supporting your people through change with compassion. By now you should be equipped to ask more and tell less, and to connect with your people human to human, not just leader to employee. Hopefully you'll also now prioritise making time to meet with your team one-on-one and see this as an essential and valuable part of your leadership toolkit.

In the next chapter, we'll tie it all together with the fifth aspect of my leading courageously through change model – the importance of committing to regular and consistent communication to ensure you maintain momentum as you steer your people through the storm.

Chapter 9

COMMIT WITH CONSISTENCY

The Five Cs

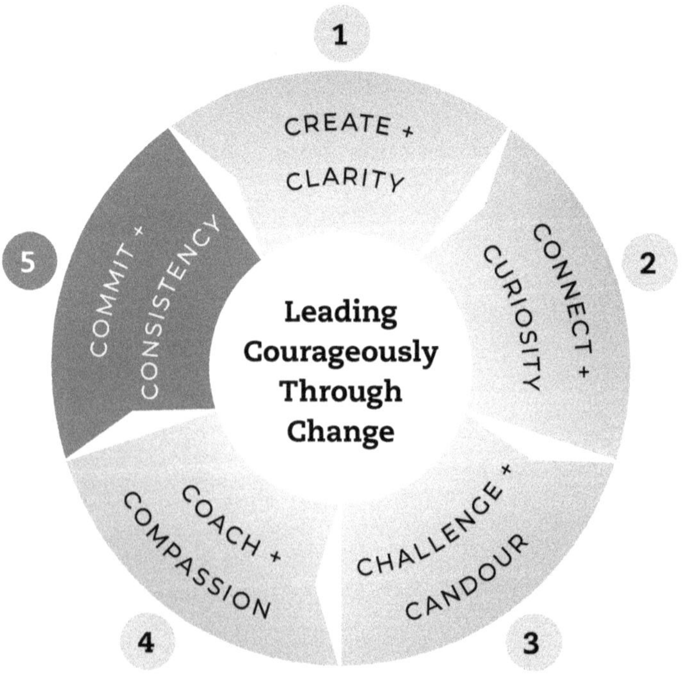

1
CREATE + CLARITY
2
CONNECT + CURIOSITY
3
CHALLENGE + CANDOUR
4
COACH + COMPASSION
5
COMMIT + CONSISTENCY
Leading Courageously Through Change

Commit: "To carry into action deliberately[...] To pledge or assign to some particular course or use."
– *Merriam-Webster Dictionary*

Consistency: "The ability to remain the same in behaviour, attitudes, or qualities." – *Macmillan Dictionary*

We've covered a lot of ground in this book and it's easy to say "Yes, yes Leah. It all makes sense. I should do that stuff".

What's harder is actually following through, doing what you say, and putting your thoughts and words into action. Knowing does not equal doing. In fact, knowing and doing are two very different things.

Committing to regular communication before, during and after a change has been implemented, and having a consistent message throughout can be challenging but is vital for helping your people to feel like they are in safe hands with you as their leader.

You may think this is absurdly obvious. You might think committing with consistency is too simple, too basic a concept to end a book like this with. But this is the one that helps ensure your people make it out the other side of change. It's also the one that often lets leaders down.

If your behaviour is erratic you will lose the trust and respect of your team.

If your messaging is unclear and you appear to backflip on decisions or contradict yourself, you'll lose the trust and respect of your team.

If you under-communicate the change or think telling your people once in an email is "job done", you'll lose the trust and respect of your team.

And once you lose these during a change (or at any time), it's very difficult to get them back and, in turn, very difficult to lead.

You need to keep banging the drum on the change message, not just say it once then set and forget. If in doubt, always err on the side of MORE communication during change, not less.

You need to be consistent in what you say to your people. That doesn't mean you can't adjust your messaging or adapt to evolving circumstances as the change unfolds or develops (COVID was a great example of where we had to do this) but it does mean you have to remain consistent and provide directional leadership, not just flip-flop like a fish, leaving your people confused.

You need to keep showing up for your team; keep showing you care – even once the change has been finalised. You need to do what you say, consistently. If you say you care, you need to show it. If you say you want feedback, you need to use it. You need to check in regularly, celebrate the wins and catch people doing the right thing if you want to reinforce good behaviour and progress. You need to commit. You need to be consistent. Let me show you how.

MORE THAN WORDS

As John P Kotter wrote in his classic book *Leading Change:* "Nothing undermines change more than behaviour by important individuals that is inconsistent with the verbal communication."

If your actions and words are misaligned, people will believe your actions every time. This can make people sceptical and distrustful of your words – which is damaging to your relationships, respect and influence as a leader. You might say all the right things but people will dismiss you as someone who simply talks the talk but doesn't walk the walk. Not only will they then lose respect for you, they'll stop listening to you too.

For example, being empathetic and supportive towards a staff member who is feeling overwhelmed by their workload means very little if you then turn around after the conversation and load them up with more tasks. Unfortunately, this is something I have seen play out repeatedly over the years and particularly during the height of COVID as organisations grappled with unprecedented change.

One government agency hired me to run a series of short online stress and self-management workshops with its regional team. The message put out by management in Melbourne was that employee wellbeing was the number one priority and the department was absolutely committed to equipping staff with the skills to look after their mental and emotional health.

The problem was the messaging completely misaligned with the reality of what was going on. It became apparent early on in the workshop that the issue wasn't people having a lack of self-management skills, it was Melbourne management having unrealistic expectations of the regional staff and refusing to make any changes to ease the overwhelming workload on people at a time when they were holding on for dear life. "Look after yourself" the spoken message was. "While we keep loading you up with more than you can handle" the action said.

The training was a success and it's always worth learning, or being reminded of, the key skills we can use to better manage ourselves in stressful situations. But to me, it was clear that my training was a tiny drop in the ocean when it came to addressing the real issue here. Following the workshops I met with regional management to brief them on what I'd heard. In this meeting, I outlined frankly where I believed the bigger problem lay. Yes, all individual staff had to take personal responsibility for managing their own health and wellbeing. But as leaders, they had a responsibility to challenge and push back against Melbourne's expectations or risk having no staff to do any of the work.

REFLECTION

1. Consider your own leadership. Are your actions and communication in alignment? Do you do what you say? Do you walk your own talk? If there's a gap (there almost always is – it's just a matter of how wide), consider what you can do to reduce it.

2. Ask yourself, what action can I take to support what I'm saying in my conversations with staff? Am I looking after my own wellbeing as I'm encouraging them to? Am I doing what I can to help them manage their challenges?

3. Look at the systems and processes you have in place. Do some of them need to change? Can you ask your company to engage career counsellors to support your people if they're going to be made redundant?

DON'T LIE TO YOURSELF

To be a great leader you have to face up to the reality of your strengths and weaknesses. You need the humility to understand that you won't always get it right, you don't know it all, and you will make mistakes. Don't beat yourself up for that – LEARN from it and do better next time.

"But I don't have time for naval gazing, Leah! I'm too busy! I'm under pressure! I have more important things to do!"

I'd argue that there's almost nothing more important than reflecting on your communication and behaviour as you lead through change. It's not optional. It's not a fluffy extra or something to push to the side.

Honest self-reflection and a commitment to aligning your actions with your words consistently is key for leading through change well.

But it can be hard. As humans and leaders we can be scared of our own shadows. We don't want to face the reality. We prefer the stories we tell ourselves instead. And boy do we get good at those.

We also judge ourselves by our intentions, not our actions. You know you're a good person who wants the best for your team, so you can become oblivious to the reality of your behaviour. You don't mean to yell when you're stressed, or get defensive and shut down other people's ideas when you're time-poor. It just happens.

It can be so easy to delude yourself, especially when you're facing a tsunami of resistance, when you get caught up in placating others, or get annoyed that things aren't going your way. You make excuses. You deny, blame and justify. You believe your own bullshit.

On the flipside, we judge other people by their actions, not their intentions (because we're not inside their mind like we are in our own), and so we don't give other people the same grace that we often (unintentionally and unconsciously) give ourselves.

When this happens, when you start believing your own rubbish, you stop leading well and others know it. Now, at this point you might be adamant this section doesn't apply to you. I really encourage you to not gloss over this and instead challenge yourself to really sit with it. I can't tell you how many leaders I've worked with who believe their own stories and are oblivious to the fact that it's bullshit in the first place.

Leaders like Ian.

Ian was cocky when he came to my workshop. All the leaders in his organisation were being put through my training and while most had come along keen to learn and be equipped with tools to help them succeed, it was clear that Ian, one of the most senior leaders in the team, thought the training was beneath him. His ego and dominant personality were on display early: he jumped in to share his own take on each point I raised and his voice dripped with superiority and condescension as he regaled us with his extensive experience leading change in his career. "I know it all," he essentially said. "I don't need to be here because I do all of this already." Mercifully for the rest of us, Ian excused himself at the morning tea break to attend to "very important business" and didn't return.

What happened when he walked out the door was immediate and intense. After a beat of silence as his colleagues watched him go, the room erupted into conversations about how full of crap Ian actually was. I haven't seen anything like it before or since. His fellow leaders didn't attempt to hide their distain.

Turns out Ian was notorious for talking the talk and saying all the right things about being a compassionate, considered and caring leader, but in practice he wasn't. In fact, he was renowned for being someone totally full of it. A man of smoke and mirrors who could put on a good front for those he wanted to impress but was completely out of touch with his people and oblivious to how he was perceived.

Ian thought he nailed courageous leadership through change. Ian was wrong. You don't want to be like Ian.

SO HOW DO YOU STOP BULLSHITTING YOURSELF?

- ▸ You build honest self-reflection as a deliberate and conscious practice into every day.
- ▸ You hold yourself to the same set of expectations and standards as you set up for your team.
- ▸ You deal with your own feelings first so you can then deal with the feelings of others.
- ▸ And, if you're really brave, you might even ask a few people that you trust, respect and admire for their feedback on your leadership.

Unless you put down your armour, face up to the reality, and take personal responsibility for your own communication and behaviour, you can never lead effectively.

ACTION

Schedule self-reflection into your day. Don't just do it once while you read this page, decide how you will make it a daily practice. Get specific. Get granular. Or it simply won't happen.

Perhaps you'll do it when you drive home from work at the end of the day. Instead of turning on the radio or a podcast, reflect on a few key questions for 10 minutes when you get in the car. Or maybe, you'll do it while you're brushing your teeth each evening. It doesn't matter when or how you do it, I just want you to make sure you schedule your reflection into your week.

If I was stripping it back to three questions to reflect on myself they would be:

1. What was it like to be around me today?
2. Did I model the behaviour I wanted to see in others?
3. What do I need to do differently tomorrow?

If you do want to take it a step further, seek feedback from a mentor or trusted colleague and check your self-reflection against their comments. You don't always have to do this but it can be a powerful "sense check" particularly if you find self-reflection on your own challenging.

COMMUNICATE EARLY, COMMUNICATE OFTEN

One of the top reasons changes fail is a lack of understanding amongst those it impacts. This under-communication by the leader and assumption that after being told once "they should know" often leads to resistance.

In Chapter 5 we spoke about the importance of creating clarity with direct, informative and simple messaging. But even if you get your messaging "right", even if you explain the why and how the change impacts them, if you don't reinforce that message consistently – if you don't commit to communicating the change in different ways, using different modes, over, and over, and over again – there is still a high chance your people will not be led through the storm.

That's why you need to communicate early and communicate

often. Get your messaging out there and then keep it out there. Don't see communication as a "tick and flick", something you do once and can then cross off your list. You need to keep banging the drum.

Brent Gleeson and Mark Owen explained this beautifully in their book *TakingPoint: A Navy SEAL's 10 Fail Safe Principles for Leading Through Change*:

"The companies that navigate change the most successfully have leaders who are constantly telling the story of the change message – both formally in meetings and casually at the water cooler. They're telling the story of progress and team accomplishments. Sending out an email written by the human resources or public relations staff and calling that communication just doesn't get it done."

Repetition reaps rewards. Sometimes – particularly if the change is complex or overwhelming – it can take multiple conversations, over an extended period of time – for the change to sink in, be understood, and ultimately (hopefully!) accepted. You may have experienced this in your own life when you've received news that has shocked you. Perhaps a bad medical diagnosis, a loved one telling you the relationship is over, or hearing about the unexpected death of a friend. In the stress of that initial moment, you don't and can't listen to what the other person is saying because the voice in your own head gets too loud. You only take in a tiny fraction of what is being said and tune out to the rest. You can't accept the news because you're not hearing it.

It takes time to process big changes. Your people may be shocked. They will have questions. They will probably be sceptical. If you don't keep repeating the message, the change can fall away as people revert to old habits and stick to what they know. Ultimate acceptance only comes with time, information and understanding.

While it can feel laboured and you'll probably worry that you're being annoying, consistent communication throughout a change gives everyone the best chance of receiving the message in a way that sinks in and penetrates. While they may not take in the message the first time, or the 10th time, eventually if it is reinforced consistently it will break through. In fact, when you start worrying that you're being annoying, you're probably close to getting the level of communication right.

But consistency doesn't just mean delivering the same message, using the same words, in the same way over and over again. Do that and your message becomes noise that people tune out to and your communication will lose its effectiveness. Rather, look for different and varied ways to present and reinforce your change message.

While consistently banging the change drum will help ensure your message is heard, mixing up the beat, and even the type of drum you use will help your people stay informed and engaged.

What follows is a list of ways you may consider communicating your change message with people throughout the process. You don't have to do all of them. Some may or may not be appropriate for you or the circumstance. But I want you to think about how you can get your message out there early and often, without relying solely on a formal or hierarchical model to communicate. I want you to look for opportunities to share and keep banging that change leadership drum.

Ways of communicating about the change:

- formal briefings (e.g., town hall briefings)
- team meetings
- pre-starts
- email
- ask-me-anything forums
- newsletters
- Q&A conversations and documents
- intranet
- daily or weekly change update huddles
- one-on-one coaching conversations
- water cooler / informal chats
- posters and hard copy notices
- conversations with informal influencers who will pass the message on.

Commit to keeping your messaging about the change fresh and consistent by communicating:

- the overview (who, what, when, where, why, how)
- updates
- progress reports
- timelines
- wins
- learnings
- myth busters
- stories

- experiences of similar changes
- answers to employee questions (Q&As)
- support avenues available to staff.

> **REFLECTION**
>
> Consider the above lists and the change you're leading through. How could you increase your communication by looking for opportunities to talk about the change more regularly? What commitments can you make?

CONSISTENCY CREATES CALM

At times of change and uncertainty everything can feel out of control. This feeling often creates stress and fear. Being a consistent presence and voice during this time can be one of the greatest gifts a leader can give their team. While everything else might be up in the air, if your staff know you will show up with an update briefing every Wednesday at 10am, this will give them a sense of security.

This was a strategy implemented by many leaders during the COVID pandemic, in particular by Victorian Premier Dan Andrews, who famously did more than 100 consecutive daily press conferences. Now, this isn't about whether you like or hate Andrews, or whether you agree with his politics or not. It's about his understanding that consistently showing up in the middle of the storm was an important part of his leadership strategy. It was as much about (if not more about) reassuring the community and providing that constant and consistent presence as it was about the actual message.

On the flipside, when you're inconsistent during change – with either the timing and frequency of your communication, or the message itself, it creates a further sense of fear, dread and confusion.

I worked with an executive team during a significant change in their organisation. According to three executive managers, who each confided in me privately, the CEO's inconsistencies made it almost impossible for them to lead their teams in a way that provided any type of stability. "He keeps flip-flopping on decisions, telling one of us one thing and then another exec something else," Kara, the finance executive said. "I don't even think he's aware that his instructions often contradict each other. It's like he forgets that he has told us different things. We don't know what the hell's going on. Even within our executive team we're not clear on what our direction is. One day we're going left and the next we're going right. It's creating chaos for us and adding to the fear of our people."

REFLECTION

Think about your own leadership through change or an emergency. Are you the consistent and stable voice that creates calm? Or the headless chook that creates chaos? If you want to be less of the second and more of the first, think about the actions you can take to ensure your messaging and the way you communicate remains consistent. Also consider how you can get on the same page as your leader colleagues to ensure your messaging is consistent with each other.

CONSISTENT DOESN'T MEAN FIXED

Ensuring your message remains consistent throughout the change process doesn't mean it has to stay fixed or that you can't evolve or adapt it over time. Change is dynamic. Even when it's a change you instigated, it rarely rolls out exactly as you planned. There are diversions along the way, pivots, potholes, roadblocks – sometimes even a "wrong way, go back" sign.

As the leader, you have to be prepared to adapt and adjust your communication along the way.

That doesn't mean you lied, it doesn't necessarily mean you got the messaging wrong (although if you did, courageous leadership would see you own this and apologise for it), it just means you need to be agile and flexible. If your message changes because the change rollout or response was tweaked, make sure you communicate the "why". All of the advice in Chapter 5 applies here – be clear, be transparent, and be visible.

CATCH PEOPLE DOING THE RIGHT THING, AND TELL THEM

One of the most important interruptions you can make in someone's day when you're a leader is to catch them doing the right thing, and then praising them for it – as specifically as possible.

While this book has largely focussed on how to lead those who are resistant or struggling through the storm of change, be careful not to only focus on addressing poor behaviour. Reinforcing and rewarding positive behaviour is far more powerful, particularly at times of high stress and change. We all want to feel valued and appreciated and in difficult times, acknowledging someone's hard work can help galvanise them to keep going and find their second wind. It can also encourage others in the team to lift too. As John F Kennedy said in a 1963 speech, "A rising tide lifts all boats."

That doesn't mean you necessarily praise your people publicly. Some won't like that. This is where knowing your people pays off. Some may prefer to be told privately, others may like the public accolades. The key is to make your feedback specific, not generic. For example, if one of your staff handles an angry customer in an empathetic way that de-escalates conflict, despite them being under the stress of change themselves, don't simply say "Good job". Rather, go with something like this:

"The way you used empathy to help that customer de-escalate was really impressive. I know things are stressful with all the changes going on right now but you took the time to listen to them and build rapport, and you also held boundaries about how they could speak to you. Well done. That's exactly the sort of customer service I want to see."

You can clearly see the difference in these approaches. One is a platitude that could be construed as condescending, the other demonstrates real appreciation and shows that you not only noticed what your staff member did, but you value the fact that they did it. You can almost guarantee the staff member will walk away thinking, "Righto, if that happens again I need to respond just like that."

On the other hand, if your people don't feel appreciated when they are under the pressure of change, they simply won't stay. They'll abandon ship or at the very least, they won't do their best work for you. Think about how you feel when your own hard work under pressure is unappreciated. It doesn't bring out the best in you, does it?

If you have children, the idea of reinforcing positive behaviour is a concept you are no doubt familiar with. And before you scoff and think that praising the positive in adults in a similar way is condescending, remember, adults, like children want to be valued and appreciated.

A new leadership team at a regional primary school inherited an exhausted, stressed and distrustful workforce. They realised that the strategies they used with their young students to reinforce positive behaviour needed to be implemented with their staff to build a positive culture too. The leaders brought the entire staff group together for a full-day workshop to reset expectations for behaviour and redefine the experience they wanted as a workgroup. A theme that came up repeatedly throughout the day was that staff wanted to feel valued, appreciated and supported.

In a follow-up workshop I ran with the senior leaders, we discussed the importance of catching people doing the right thing and telling them so as to reinforce the behaviours. I asked the leaders to think about how they might do this. They decided to start handwriting thank you notes to staff when they noticed them upholding the new agreed behaviours, specifically acknowledging what it was they saw. The leaders would then leave these notes in the staff member's pigeonhole for them to discover. This simple, quiet, small action packed a big punch. These unexpected notes were highly valued and made staff more determined to continue changing their mindset, actions and behaviour.

CELEBRATE THE WINS – BIG AND SMALL

Change is exhausting. It can feel like it's never-ending – particularly if it's a big change that will take years to transition to, embed or implement. While keeping your eyes on the prize of the final vision or destination is important, so is celebrating the little wins along the way.

One of your many challenges when leading people through

change is to keep your people engaged. You can't do that if they feel overwhelmed and like they're never going to get there. If the end goal appears unachievable and unreachable your people will likely become discouraged. If you don't acknowledge and celebrate the process and the small achievements along the way, don't be surprised when your people lose motivation and interest.

Celebrating the small wins can motivate, inspire and relieve stress. It helps people to feel appreciated and valued for the often-difficult work they are doing to adopt a change.

It can increase faith that the effort is worth it and encourage others to commit to the change. And crucially it can also help sway the cynics if they see real progress. Motivation follows action, not the other way around. If your people see progress, they are much more likely to get on board.

If this was a change management book, I would write about breaking the change down into small chunks and achievable goals from a task perspective. But because this is a change leadership book, I'm not focussed on the practicalities of that. Rather, I'm focussed on how you as the leader look for and highlight progress and wins along the way. Remember, this is about the people bit. And people have a negative bias. As the leader, you have a responsibility to bring the positives to the fore. This will likely take conscious effort because you have a negative bias too. Just like catching people doing the right thing and acknowledging it, celebrating the wins is something that requires your focus, commitment and consistency. Think about how you can build this reflection of looking for and celebrating the wins into your leadership practice.

All progress is a win. It doesn't have to be a big milestone you're celebrating, it can be something small. The key is to recognise and acknowledge progress in the right direction. Not only does this give people a boost and dopamine hit, it also provides you with fresh content to communicate so that you can keep banging the change drum with consistency.

Don't just look for the big and obvious milestones set out by the CEO or official change leaders in your organisation either. Look for the wins that your team achieves and highlight them specifically.

Each celebration doesn't have to be a big one. I'm not suggesting you hire a marching band and throw confetti every time you get something right. Simply acknowledging the progress can be celebration enough.

Here are some ways you might like to celebrate the small wins along the way:

- ► Acknowledge the progress in normal communication such as meetings, newsletters and one-on-one conversations.
- ► Have a morning tea or shout everyone coffee.
- ► Write thank you notes to those who contributed to the win.
- ► Tell your team they can knock off a couple of hours early.
- ► Tell other people in your business about the wins in your team.

1. Create a timeline of the change and how it affects your team. Map out small milestones you can celebrate along the way.

2. Think about what constitutes a "win" in the way your team navigates the change. You may even want to involve them in this process. Make a commitment to celebrating these wins consistently.

3. Look for and acknowledge the wins. Make this a conscious practice. Don't let it fall away.

SUMMARY

Remember those old movies set on the high seas where the captain or first mate on the ship had to yell "heave" to the crew repeatedly as they raised the sails, or "row" as they pulled the oars? That's what this chapter was about and what you have to do in your role as a leader if you want to support your team to steer through the storm of change. You have to commit to being consistent in your message, your behaviour and your actions if you want to make it through to calmer waters.

In this chapter you have learned the importance of staying true to you and your word, being accountable for your own behaviour, banging the change drum, showing your appreciation, and celebrating the wins of change with your team.

You need to keep your people pulling in the same direction and if you're not consistent and committed, that effort can fade away.

Words and intentions written on a page, or thoughts in your brain are nice, but it's only actions that make a difference. Knowing is not doing. It's time for you to steer the ship.

CONCLUSION

It was Greek philosopher Heraclitus who said, "The only constant in life is change," more than 2,500 years ago. This quote has stood the test of time for good reason: it's true.

Change will happen to your industry, your organisation and your team whether you like it or not. While you can't control a lot of what happens, as a leader you have a chance to influence how your people get through it. You can't do it for them (no one person can row the boat) but you can steer them in the right direction.

You can help your people navigate the stormy seas. You can help to reduce people's pain and suffering. You can increase the chance of the change being successful. And you can use the experience to improve your credibility and skill as a leader.

As you've learned throughout this book, leading through change is about people and to do it well you have to use your people skills. Working with humans requires you to bring your humanity. Dealing with the feelings and connecting with your team is not optional, it's essential if you want to make it out the other side.

To do that, you need to **create clarity** and give people the simple and clear messaging they need to understand what is happening, what it means for them, and why the change is so important.

You also need to **connect with curiosity** to ensure your people feel seen and heard. You need to check in, empathise with their experience and ask more questions to understand their point of view.

Only once you have connected can you expect to be able to **challenge with candour** and have any success in urging your people to choose their response, so they can still deliver on outcomes and behave appropriately under pressure.

This "tough love" needs to be countered again with the warmth of **coaching with compassion** at a one-on-one level to help your people.

And finally, you need to keep banging the drum. You need to **commit with consistency** in your communication, behaviour and actions if you want to build trust so your people follow you through the storm.

It's these Five Cs together in continuous motion throughout the change, not linear one-off progression, that will help you lead your people courageously through.

You have the power to help your team weather the storm and now you've read this book you're equipped with more skills, strategies, scripts and structure to help you do it. You have the chance to help your team build their capacity for adaptability and resilience under pressure. You have the chance to build your own standing as a leader. You have the opportunity to prove that you can get results from your team even when things are uncertain. You have the chance to imagine and create your – and your team's – future.

Picture this: change is happening and your people are processing and working their way through it. They are not stuck or bogged down resisting, blocking or arguing against the change. They have not given up in dismay and they are not running around like headless chooks. Sure, they may not like the change and they may still raise their concerns and advocate on key points, and that's ok. Different opinions are ok! But they're working their way through it with you, not against you. They are processing their feelings, choosing their response, they are still able to function, do their work, and be a productive team. Those who can't have elected, or been led by you, to leave. That's ok too. Losing people along the way is not necessarily a bad outcome. Sometimes it's for the best.

Those who remain stand with you and trust you to steer them through the storm because that's what you're doing – STEERING. You're not a steamroller and you're not a shirker. You are modelling the behaviour you want to see in your people and, as a result, they are modelling what they see back to you. You're taking personal responsibility for your leadership and your team understands they have personal responsibility for their response too. It doesn't make navigating the change easy or mean it's going to be smooth sailing, but making it through to the other side is possible if you are all pulling in the same direction. Imagine how good it will feel when you break through the storm and emerge back into the sun?

Before I sign off and end this book, I want to make sure that I'm setting you up for success and to do that I want to flag three final risks to avoid after reading this book. I want to leave you with similar advice to that which I gave at the end of *Soft is the New Hard*. Advice that I give at the end of every workshop.

RISKS TO AVOID WHEN YOU FINISH THIS BOOK

You mistake knowing for doing.

- ► Reading this book will equip you with the skills and strategies to lead your people courageously through change but knowing does not equal doing. Being able to spout off the strategies to others means very little. It's the action you take – personally and professionally – based on your learnings that is important.

You get overwhelmed and don't know where to start, so you do nothing.

- ► As I said right back in the introduction, improving your leadership through change is a big project and one of the biggest mistakes you can make is to try to do it all at once.

Start small and remember, developing any new skill takes time. Break the strategies in this book down into small, manageable chunks and then break them down further into tangible actions. Pick one or two things to focus on initially, get conscious of them, make a commitment and hold yourself accountable for doing them, and only then move onto adding in another strategy.

You doubt your capabilities at putting the learnings into practice, or try something once and it doesn't go well so you give up.

▸ No one gets it right all the time. Communication and leadership are not something you'll ever perfect. BUT they are something everyone can improve – if you're willing to learn and if you're willing to do the work. I don't care whether you're a seasoned leader with huge experience leading through change, or a new people leader recently promoted to your first role, everyone can do better – including me and I teach this stuff for a living and literally wrote the book!

The only way to get better is to be humble enough to admit this, self-aware enough to know the areas you need to work on, and persistent enough to strive for continual improvement. That means practice. Experiment. Try new things, learn from your mistakes, and then try again. You're not going to nail it all first go and you're not going to change your own habits and natural tendencies in five minutes. As you know from reading this book, making change and having it stick takes time and commitment.

So, how do you do it? How can you have the best chance of successfully implementing the strategies in this book and developing your leadership?

1. Make a commitment. Commit to learning and improving. Commit to putting your learnings into action.

2. Increase your self-awareness and get conscious of how you communicate and lead now (there is a communication style questionnaire in my first book and available as a free download on my website that can help with this at leahmether.com.au).

3. Identify your opportunities for improvement.

4. Start small. Pick one or two things to focus on initially.

5. Be accountable. Tell someone what you're working on and ask them to check in.

6. Persist and practice. To make real and lasting change to your communication and leadership you need to be ferociously persistent. Start by practising in low-threat, low-stakes environments if you can. And keep trying even when it feels too hard.

You have the foundations you need in this book to help you communicate with and lead your team courageously through whatever change you next face. I hope these foundations hold you in good stead and provide the map you need to navigate you and your people through.

My wish is for a world in which all leaders step up to the challenge of leading with humanity and dealing with the feelings of their people in order to steer them through the inevitable storm of change.

We may not be able to control the weather but we can always choose how we respond. Choose wisely.

WANT TAILORED SUPPORT?

This book gives you the structure, skills and strategies to lead your team courageously through change.

It is written for a general leadership audience and as such does not necessarily provide the tailored support you need to navigate through your particular storm.

That's where my in-house workshops and programs come in.

If you want support to apply The Five Cs® of Leading Courageously Through Change to a specific change or leadership group in your organisation, get in touch.

I'd love to help you steer your people through to calmer waters.

Visit my website at **leahmether.com.au**
Phone: **1300 532 461**
Email: **support@leahmether.com.au**

ACKNOWLEDGMENTS

This book is essentially a love letter to the leaders of Gippsland.

I first had the idea for it in 2019, not long after the publication of my first book *Soft is the New Hard: How to Communicate Effectively Under Pressure.*

I wanted to write it to help leaders in my region navigate the enormous changes of power and timber industry transitions.

While *Soft is the New Hard* laid out the foundations that underpin effective communication and leadership, I could see the next step was equipping leaders with the skills to navigate the disruptive change that was on the horizon.

Little did I know the biggest industry disruption we'd ever experienced across the globe was about to hit us all.

When COVID-19 hit in 2020, leaders around the world – be they in business, organisations, politics, community groups or families – were thrust into the midst of unprecedented change and disruption.

No one was prepared and everyone was winging it.

Some leaders did it well, steering their people through with courage. Others faltered. Not because they were bad humans or even poor leaders, but in the face of such overwhelming change they were not equipped with the skills to lead.

This book aims to ensure leaders are not in that position again.

I wrote *Steer Through the Storm* as I navigated the storm of change in my own life. As such, the fact that it now sits completed and published is one of my proudest achievements.

Seeing my hard work, persistence, determination, late nights and early mornings reflected in these pages gives me an overwhelming sense of joy and satisfaction – even more so than with my first book.

But I didn't get this book to where it is on my own. I had wonderful support, and those people need to be acknowledged.

First, I'd like to thank my book coach extraordinaire Kath Walters who again helped guide me through the planning process.

Kath's structure, guidance and frank feedback ensured I had a detailed book outline before I wrote the first word of the draft. Thanks Kath, it was such a pleasure to work with you for a second time.

Next up is my editor, Lu Sexton. You are awesome. Thank you for helping me tighten and refine my manuscript. Your suggestions and eagle eye were invaluable.

To my first readers, Janine Garner, Maree McPherson, Tanya Heaney-Voogt, Ron Mether, Marg Mether, David Burt, Sally Neenan and Kelly Mether – thank you for generously giving me your time and valuable feedback. It made the book so much better.

Stephanie Preston from The Preston Edit. Thank you for your impeccable attention to detail as my proofreader.

Liz Seymour from Seymour Designs – you nailed the cover design and layout for me again. Thanks Liz, you are brilliant at what you do.

In addition to being available as a paperback and e-book, *Steer Through the Storm* is also available as an audiobook, thanks to the help of Dave Stokes from author2audio.

This book contains references to the works of many great thought leaders. In particular, I'd like to acknowledge the models and concepts of Brené Brown, Sue Langley, Stephen Karpman, David Emerald, Daniel Goleman, Amy Cuddy, Viktor Frankl, Stephen Covey, Geoffrey Roberts, and my friend Tanya Heaney-Voogt.

These pages include many stories and anecdotes from a wide range of clients: leaders who have shared their fears, successes, failures, learnings and insecurities with me over many years. Although I have changed most of their names and identifying details, their stories are real. Thank you all for your questions, vulnerability and desire to improve your leadership and communication.

To my team – Mel and Efriel – thank you for helping me create space in my business to write.

And last but most importantly, to my family and friends. I simply could not have written this book without your love and support.

To my parents, Ron and Marg, words really can't express how wonderful you are. I could not do the work that I do without you. Thank you for being such great leadership role models, as well as the best parents, grandparents, babysitters, lawnmowers and garden ninjas going around. I appreciate everything you do for me.

To my sisters, Kelly, Rachael and Jessica. Thank you for always being there for me, particularly while I wrote this book. All three of you are incredible leaders in your own right and I love watching you make a difference in the world. Your workplaces are lucky to have you.

To my great mates Mia, Kate, Katie and Gaz. You four deserve a medal. Thanks for being my safe place through both the laughs and the tears as I navigated my storm.

And finally, to my sons – Sam, Callum and Lucas. Leading you is both my greatest joy and challenge in life. I hope I steer you well.

Life is good and storm clouds pass.

Here comes the sun.

www.ingramcontent.com/pod-product-compliance
Lightning Source LLC
Chambersburg PA
CBHW041255040426
42334CB00028BA/3027